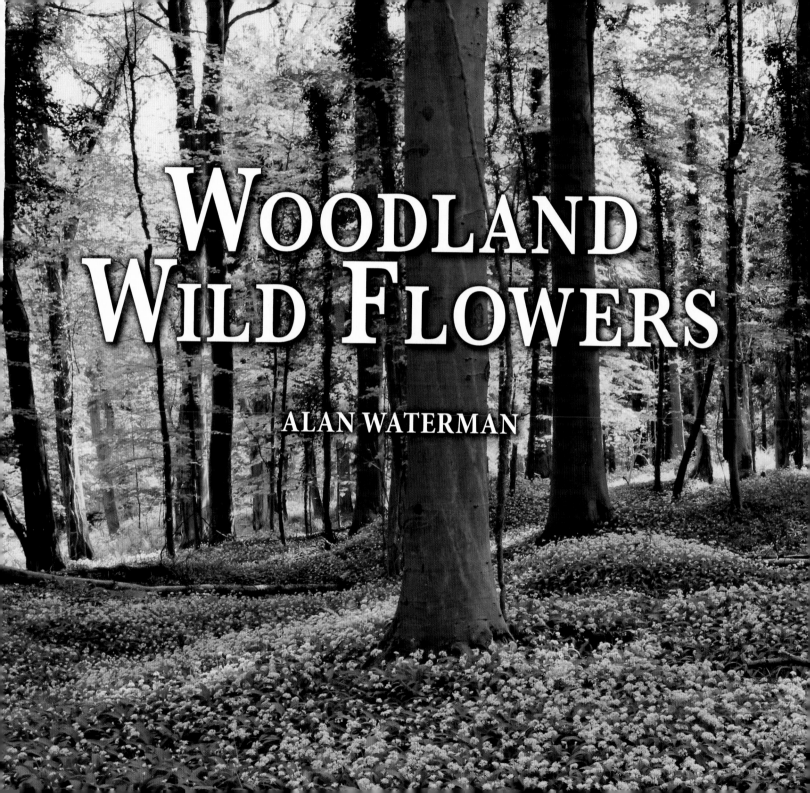

WOODLAND WILD FLOWERS

ALAN WATERMAN

First published in Great Britain by Merlin Unwin Books Ltd, 2021

Merlin Unwin Books Ltd
Palmers House
7 Corve Street
Ludlow
Shropshire SY8 1DB   UK

www.merlinunwin.co.uk
The author asserts his moral right to be identified with this work.

ISBN 978-1-913159-25-2
Designed by Jo Dovey, Ludlow
Printed by Leo Paper Products

To Anita
My endless gratitude

Photo credits

All the photos in this book are taken by Alan Waterman except those listed below. Alan expresses his gratitude to the following people who have kindly contributed photos, and also to any fellow-enthusiasts who pointed him to the location of certain flowers:

Yellow Star of Bethlehem page 35 © Andrew Skinner
Spanish Bluebell page 55 © Shutterstock
Leopardsbane page 89 © Ruth Hyslop
White Helleborine page 138 © Julian Clinkard
Red Helleborine page 139 © Julian Clinkard
Violet Helleborine page 165 © Julian Clinkard
Common Wintergreen p.169 and back cover © Ian Green
Pale Willowherb page 175 © Ian Green
Green Helleborine p197 © Dawn & James Langiewicz

CONTENTS

Welsh Poppy

AUTHOR'S PREFACE

Ninewells Wood. I have much for which to thank this wood and one of those things is the development of this book.

I live in a picturesque Gloucestershire village between the Wye Valley and the Forest of Dean. Soon after my wife and I moved here in 2013, we also became the proud owners of six and a half acres of Welsh woodland, only about 7 miles from where we live. It was not the most attractive of woodland when we bought it. It was a plantation of Corsican Pines, rows and rows of them, which made the wood dark and boring. There were a few deciduous trees but they were struggling to survive against the stranglehold of the conifers and as a result they were very tall, thin and straggly. They were mostly Oak and Silver Birch with a few Beech and Rowan. At the edge of the wood there were a few more substantial Oaks and Beech, and a few woodland wild flowers: some Bluebells, Wood Anemones and even some Wood Sorrel. But mostly the wood was dark and all that grew in the interior were ferns, predominantly bracken, and some nasty brambles which were very adept at tripping one up.

It was our intention to gradually improve the wood by cutting down some of the conifers ourselves and creating little patches of light where flowers might grow – naive amateurs!

It was a Plantation Ancient Woodland Site (PAWS), which means that it has had trees growing on it continuously since 1800. At some stage it was converted into a conifer plantation. It was probably first planted up with conifers in about 1920 and then felled in about 1965 and replanted with the Corsican Pines which were growing there when we purchased it, so there had been two generations of conifers.

Ninewells Wood, of which we bought only a small part, covers an area of about 100 acres and is in multiple ownership. The largest area belongs to Natural Resources Wales. Prior to moving to Gloucestershire, I had owned and run a Field Study Centre in Norfolk. I thought I knew a bit about forestry. I put the poor condition of the Corsican Pines, which made up the majority of trees in my 'new' wood, down to the fact that they had not been thinned out – as is normal practice when they reach 20-25 years of age – and then they had not been felled when they had reached 40 years of age. So we had trees which were growing too close together, were too big and were thus suffering. A few were actually dead.

After a short while we decided to get some advice from a professional company, as we were beginning to realise that there may be a bit more involved in managing our wood than just chopping down the odd tree here and there.

A woodland management expert duly visited our wood and fairly quickly spotted that our trees were infected with the fungal disease *dothistroma*. Apparently most Corsican Pines have this disease, which causes the needles to fall off, and each year the new needles become infected and fall off, so in effect there is only ever one year's worth of needles on the tree at any one time, which makes the canopy look sparse.

DEFRA do not need to be notified of the presence of the disease if the trees are in an established woodland and one is not obliged to fell the trees as is the case with some other tree diseases. I think the authorities recognise that nothing can be done to prevent it killing virtually all Corsican Pines and that there is no great sentiment regarding this species. They simply have value as a short-lived commercial tree. The problem lies in the fact that one does not want it spreading to the native Scot's Pine in the Caledonian Forests of Scotland.

The end result of the disease is that after a few years the tree dies. A few years after that, the timber will only be saleable as a source of biofuel, before it totally rots away.

Our expert suggested that the best way to return our woods to something like an ancient woodland and definitely the most commercially viable course of action would be to clear fell, and start again.

We followed the expert's advice and our woodland was chopped down, the logs were stacked up – piles and piles of them – and lorries came and took them away. There were three grades of timber. The logs with the largest diameter were used for timber to make such things as joists and floor boards. The next size logs were for 'biofuel'. The smallest logs were used for fencing, fence posts and the 'larchlap' fence panels that surround most urban gardens. The whole process took about six weeks from start to finish, the finish consisting of a man with a JCB spending five days scraping up all the brash into huge bonfire piles, some of which were set alight. Not all the brash piles were burnt because the wind changed direction after he had been working for a couple of days and further burning would have run the risk of setting fire to neighbouring woodland and of smoking out two nearby houses. So the brash piles remaining at that point were left and whilst they initially looked unsightly, they soon began to rot down and have now blended in and provide a good micro-habitat for all sorts of life.

The process involved in chopping down a tree nowadays is a technological miracle carried out by a very expensive and sophisticated machine. From a living growing tree to half a dozen logs lying on the ground takes about forty seconds.

The tree felling and clearing process took place in the spring and early summer and amazingly by that autumn the first tiny seedlings of Silver Birch and Gorse were starting to make their appearance. The Gorse seeds must have been lying dormant in the soil for the last fifty years or so, as there was no Gorse in the wood when we purchased it. I was keen to see what other new species might spring up. From the outset I set about recording what I saw there and what I was doing. It was a diary which included a lot of photographs.

At first there were just a few wild flowers, especially around the edges where some light did filter in. I subdivided my recordings into categories such as birds, butterflies and other invertebrates, fungi and of course wild flowers. The typical woodland wild flowers such as Bluebells, Wood Anemones and Wood Sorrel which had originally been seen were quickly joined by new species appearing such as Foxgloves, and two species of Heather (mainly Ling but also some Bell Heather). There was a lot of the Sorrel related to Dock, together with St John's Wort, Red Campion, Stitchwort and even a Ragged Robin.

I also visited many other woodlands, all over Britain, and this led to the wild flower list being extended. It was at this point that the idea of a book about woodland wild flowers was formed.

Spending time in the countryside has become increasingly popular and spending time in woodlands especially so. It is now recognised that the benefits of time spent in a wood are wide-ranging, for mind, body and spirit.

Our woodland is now classified by the Forestry Commission as a Recovering Ancient Woodland Site (RAWS) – no longer PAWS. To my mind it is recovering quite quickly. Within a couple of years of felling, the little Silver Birches which sprang up just weeks after the clear fell were well above head height, and a year or so later needed thinning to allow others to develop into good strong trees. The few tall spindly deciduous trees that I had saved from the automated lumberjack machine largely survived. A few did succumb to the wind but most enjoyed the freedom offered by more light and good soil, and relatively quickly they thickened up and started to spread some horizontal branches. In terms of wild flowers, things also moved on. We had quite a show of Foxgloves in the years immediately after the felling but subsequently they subsided. The Bluebells looked better every year and some individuals made their appearance in regions well away from the main populations. The Wood Sorrel was one casualty of the felling, but all in all recovery was soon underway. Should I live to be a hundred then it will be good to see what is achieved – not an ancient woodland but I believe something approaching that.

Alan Waterman
January 2021

Greater Stitchwort

Wood Spurge

EARLY SPRING

(MARCH AND APRIL)

In March and April the plants of the woodland and hedgerows burst into flower, often brightly coloured. This is the time of year when the woodland plants that rely on insects as their pollinators have the best chance to attract them. Most insects head towards light and avoid dark places, so with the minimal leaf cover of early spring, the woods are bright, in spite of the shorter day length.

Some species, such as Wild Daffodils, Cuckooflowers, Ramsons and of course Bluebells make quite a dazzling visual display too which further improves the chances of attracting pollinators. Other species hitch a ride on the backs of these more dominant species, so in amongst the Bluebells one may find a few Early Purple Orchids or better still a Fly Orchid. The dominant, early spring woodland flowers are nearly all perennials, which increases their chances of survival. Many of the plants that flower at this time of year have a fairly short season. Woods can be radiant blue with Bluebells one week and even a couple of weeks later the flowers are all but gone. There are a few species such as Gorse, which flower for an extended period but even they are at their peak in early spring.

Most of the woodland plants flowering at this time of the year rely on a good store of food, laid down the previous year, so they have bulbs, corms or rhizomes rich in starch which can be converted quickly into sugars and then used to propel their flowers skyward in the hope of attracting the required insects.

Some species have very specific requirements in terms of pollinators. An extreme example is Lords and Ladies which relies on one tiny species of fly. Several of the Orchids are also quite specific but in the case of others, such as the Buttercup, anything crawling over the surface will effect pollination. Even a slug or snail will be quite up to the task.

SPRING CROCUS

Crocus vernus

Spring Crocus

There are many species of Crocus and even more cultivars. *Crocus vernus* has been with us and naturalised for a long time. It is recorded in books in the 17th century, and even in those days there were several different varieties.

Crocus vernus is the blue or purple-blue flowered Crocus, as opposed to the yellow ones which may be *Crocus flavus*; or *Crocus chrysanthus* which can be yellow or creamy white. The Crocus genus is a bit of a nightmare as there are over thirty different species and a vast number of different cultivars.

The native Spring Crocus is quite plain and rather thin. Over the years, bolder forms have been developed, which have stronger colour and a more substantial shape. Some have a less uniform colour, including two-tone stripes and white lines. Inkpen in Berkshire is a famous crocus site where there are hundreds of them, naturalised, beautiful and visited regularly.

The Spring Crocus was introduced into cultivation in Britain before 1600 and was first recorded in the wild in 1763. It may once have been cultivated to produce a substitute for saffron.

CREEPING COMFREY

Symphytum grandiflorum

Norfolk and used to regularly harvest the leaves and plunge them into a large bucket of water. Six weeks later it was ripe and smelly, a rich brown liquid which I would carefully pour into a watering can, and then dilute it with rain from the water butt so that it was about 10% strength. The result was tea coloured and still quite pungent and I would water it onto crops such as tomatoes, aubergines and green peppers.

The crops were prolific!

...turning blue a little later

There are several species of Comfrey, but there are just two that one might come across in woodlands or shady locations. One is Creeping Comfrey *Symphytum grandiflorum*, which flowers in mid-March, and continues to flower right through spring and summer. The other is Tuberous Comfrey *Symphytum tuberosum* which comes into flower in June and July.

Creeping Comfrey, also known as Dwarf Comfrey, is often found close to water, low growing and carpeting the ground. It has rhizomes which gradually spread out, so a small patch can become quite invasive eventually. The sparse flowers are arranged in a one-sided spike. It typically has 10-15 individual flowers which are cream or white, but pink or purple when in bud. The leaves have a stalk (petiole), so the leaf blade does not run down and fuse with the stalk.

Creeping Comfrey is not a native species but has become naturalised. Originally it came from the Caucasus and is very much restricted at present to the southern counties of Britain.

Pink when first in bloom...

Tuberous Comfrey is mostly found in Scotland, where it favours damp, shady woodlands, but it also grows in hedgerows and roadside verges. The flowers are creamy white, and the leaf blade continues down the stem, in a winged effect.

It is well known that Comfrey is good in compost and can be used as a fertiliser. I had some growing in my garden in

GORSE

Ulex europaeus

I have included Gorse as an early flowering plant, but it normally continues to flower all year round, as suggested in *The Song of The Gorse Fairies* by Cicely Mary Barker:

'When gorse is out of blossom,'
(Its prickles bare of gold)
'Then kissing's out of fashion,'
Said country-folk of old.

Gorse is also known as Furze. The peak of flowering is normally in May and by midsummer the bushes have lots of short seed pods.

Gorse is a member of the pea family. This family is huge, from small plants such as vetches through to the familiar beans and peas, to bushes such as Gorse and Broom and even trees such as Laburnum and False Acacia. All of these plants have nodules on their roots which contain bacteria that can convert atmospheric nitrogen into nitrogenous fertiliser and this is of benefit not only to the bacteria but also to the host plants so these plants can often survive in areas low in natural fertiliser, where they can out-compete plants which do not have this advantage. Gorse can therefore colonise heathlands and moorlands which are low in nutrients.

In my wood when I first bought it, there was no Gorse although there was some in the more open areas nearby. We felled all the Corsican Pines when we bought the wood and within a couple of months, Gorse plants were popping up everywhere. There had obviously been a vast seed bank of them in the soil waiting for good times to return. They

Gorse

sprang up, particularly on the edges of the bonfire sites where the brash had been burnt. This is because Gorse seeds have a tough seed coat and they either have to wait many years for this to decompose naturally, or they speed up the process by having the seed coat cracked by heat. The distance from the heat source is critical because if the seeds are too close, the seed inside is cooked and if too far away, the seed coat will not split. So one often sees a narrow band of Gorse plants growing up around the edge of a bonfire site.

Gorse is a favoured food of rabbits, and the little Gorse plants in our wood were soon regularly nibbled back. Eventually they grew up above the level where a rabbit could reach and reached full size, which is about 2-3m in height. How quickly this can happen in a wood depends on how many rabbits there are and how much alternative food there is. In an area in Norfolk called Syderstone Common, for instance, the rabbits moulded the Gorse bushes into peculiar low topiary shapes, none more than 50cm high, nor did they flower. Gorse is sometimes host to the parasitic plant Broomrape which takes its food and water from other species. There are several species of Broomrape but the most common one lives on Broom and Gorse. The species which sometimes occurs in woodlands is Ivy Broomrape because it parasitises Ivy but this is a fairly rare species.

Where Gorse flowers, the air has a strong smell of coconuts, especially on warm sunny days. It smells like a tropical beach with lots of sunbathers slapping on the coconut sun oil. A few weeks later the seed pods will have developed. These are typical pea- or bean-like pods but they are short and most contain just three or four seeds. Many of these seeds have a small grub living in them, the gorse seed weevil, so only a small number of the seeds are viable. The seeds are dispersed by the seed pod violently splitting in two lengthways, whilst at the same time twisting up so that the seeds are flung out. This process creates a little cracking noise and on hot days in July they can be heard as they go off.

Another interesting insect associated with Gorse is a beautiful little butterfly, the Green Hairstreak. The caterpillar of this butterfly feeds on Gorse as well as other plants.

Gorse in Ninewells Wood, Monmouthshire

Barren Strawberry

BARREN STRAWBERRY

Potentilla sterilis

This little plant flowers from the beginning of March onward but because it is small it is easily overlooked.

The Barren Strawberry has five little white petals just like the Wild Strawberry but there is a gap between each petal, whereas the petals of the Wild Strawberry join together at the base and although they are not actually fused, there is no gap. The blue-green leaves of the Barren Strawberry are hairy, especially on the underside, and there is a little point at the apex which is smaller than the points either side of it, unlike the leaf of the Wild Strawberry. Although the flower has five petals, it has ten sepals that are arranged in two whorls of five.

Obviously, given the name, they do not produce little strawberries and the seeds are dry and brown. However, I am not particularly impressed by the wild strawberries produced by *Fragaria vesca*. I do not find them tasty and it takes ages to collect enough to make even a small dessert. In my humble opinion it is really not worth it; better to leave them for the wood mice and birds.

These plants are often found growing on the edge of woodlands on banks and dry places and on the tops of drystone walls. They are common and continue flowering until May.

GREATER PERIWINKLE
Vinca major

and

LESSER PERIWINKLE
Vinca minor

Greater Periwinkle

The Greater Periwinkle is a recognised garden and woodland plant, albeit an introduced species. It was first recorded in the wild in 1650 in Middlesex.

It flowers in most months but is most prolific in the spring. It will happily grow in shady and fairly damp places, often along paths.

It is quick to colonise, and a few stems of it in moist soil will soon establish it. The plant is perennial, so once established, it is there more or less for good. It produces seed and can spread this way as well.

The Lesser Periwinkle has smaller flowers, 25-30mm diameter, whereas the flowers of the Greater Periwinkle are normally about 35mm across. If you look very carefully at the edge of the leaves and the sepals, the Greater Periwinkle has little white hairs on them, and those of the Lesser Periwinkle will not.

Lesser Periwinkle

VIOLETS:
SWEET, COMMON DOG and EARLY DOG

Viola odorata, Viola riviniana and Viola reichenbachiana

Common Dog Violet

after the petals have died and surround the developing seed pod. Sepals can either end in a long narrow point or they can be rounded. This is important. In the photograph below the sepals are easy to see and are quite obviously pointed, so not a Sweet Violet. Blunt, rounded sepals indicate that the species is the Sweet Violet. There is also a white form of this species which is often seen.

Violets all have a spur which protrudes behind the flower. The nectar is produced at the base of the spur and bees insert their proboscis down the spur to access it. Slugs have learnt that if you nibble a hole in

Early Dog Violet showing the dark purple spur

Early Dog Violet

There are several species of Violet, of which three are found in woodland, and at a casual glance they all look similar. They flower from early March onwards.

In woodlands and shady places it is possible to come across all three different species: Sweet Violet, Common Dog Violet, and Early Dog Violet, also sometimes called Wood Dog Violet.

To tell the difference between them, it is necessary to look closely at the flowers and know a little about the flower structure. Behind the petals there are green sepals which protect the flower whilst in bud. In the case of Violets, the sepals remain the back of the spur you get direct access to this food source! The spur can be the same colour as the petals, or it may be darker, and this is perhaps the most important distinguishing feature. There may also be a groove running along the length of it. A key visual identification is to look to see if the groove extends beyond the end of the spur, so that as one looks at the end of the spur, it appears notched. This would suggest that it is the Common Dog Violet. In shape, it is a shorter, fatter, baggier spur, whereas a longer narrower spur suggests Early Dog Violet. If one has good eyesight or a hand lens, the little appendages at the top of the sepals are larger in the Common Dog Violet than in Early Dog Violet.

Finally, one needs to look for stolons, commonly known as runners. Stolons enable violets to spread, much like strawberries do. Look for stolons as another identification aid. Here is a checklist of woodland Violet indicators.

Sweet Violet: sepals blunt, spur same colour, runners present.
Common Dog Violet: sepals pointed, spur same colour, runners absent.
Early Dog Violet: sepals pointed, spur darker, runners absent.

There are several hybrids including the Hairy Dog Violet which crosses with the Sweet Violet; the Teesdale Dog Violet which crosses with the Common Dog Violet, and crosses between the Early and the Common Dog Violet, just to complicate things.

Sweet Violet

Finally, the reason for the name 'Dog' is because it does not smell sweet. Most Sweet Violets really do smell sweet.

Sweet Violet

Wood Spurge

WOOD SPURGE

Euphorbia amygdaloides

Wood Spurge is not one of the most exciting woodland wild flowers one is likely to encounter. Its flowers are green, a lighter fresher colour than the leaves, which tend to be dark blue-green. The stems often appear blood red. It is a flower which is quite easy to overlook.

It flowers early in the year, at the same time as Wood Anemones and just before the trees get their leaves in early March through to May. The flowers themselves are very small. What makes the 'show' are bracts which form a cup that the flower sits in.

Wood Spurge is unlike most woodland plants in that it overwinters with its leaves on and not as a bulb, corm or rhizome, tucked up underground. This has the advantage that it can make use of the light, and photosynthesise throughout the winter, as long as it is just warm enough and not covered with snow. This may be the reason for its more southerly distribution. It is not widely distributed elsewhere.

Numerous plant nurseries offer its many cultivars for sale, such as *Euphorbia amygdaloides* 'Purpurea' which has bracts which are tinted purple. Gardeners like it because it will grow in the shady and 'unloved' spaces where other plants will not. However, as is often the case, these garden varieties then find their way into the wild and breed with the native population.

Wood Spurge produces a white sticky liquid when the leaves or stems are damaged, broken or picked. This is poisonous and will cause a great deal of pain and inflammation if it gets into your eyes, mouth, a cut, or any other regions so be warned! Best to leave it alone and not to pick it. I was told by a local gamekeeper that poachers and country folk would use it to catch fish. A bundle of it was gathered and then bruised and placed in a pond. The fish would then be paralysed and rise to the surface, and the good ones could be selected and taken home for cooking.

COLTSFOOT
Tussilago farfara

W hen established, Coltsfoot can thrive in woodlands, although it is not solely a woodland plant and it can be found growing in a variety of places.

They flower early and usually produce their flowers before the leaves. The flowers are typical Compositae with yellow ray florets and yellow central disc florets. The very base of each ray floret is a slightly paler yellow, so it produces a light, almost white circle, around the central disc. Although the flowers look similar to Dandelions, Coltsfoot is more closely related to Groundsel and is in the Aster family. The flower closely resembles the garden Aster except that it is yellow not purple.

The leaves are large and light green on top with a very hairy, grey underside. They appear just as the flowers are fading (from whence comes one of its old common names 'Son before Father') and the leaves continue growing throughout the spring and early summer months. They are eventually large enough to be mistaken for Butterbur. As the leaves develop, the seed heads can be seen. These are white tufts of fluffy wind-dispersed seeds.

Coltsfoot

OPPOSITE-LEAVED SAXIFRAGE

Chrysosplenium oppositifolium
and Alternate-leaved Saxifrage *Chrysosplenium alternifolium*

These two species of Saxifrage are similar, the main difference being fairly obvious in the names: one has its leaves in pairs and the other has them attached singly up the stem. Sometimes they are referred to as Golden Saxifrage and Alternate-leaved Golden Saxifrage. The Opposite-leaved species is by far the more common of the two. They flower from early March through to May.

Golden Saxifrage grows in various locations. It prefers wet areas, often growing along the sides of tracks where puddles develop after heavy rain or in wet boggy woods next to streams. It seems tolerant of heavy shade but, as it only grows to a height of a few centimetres, it cannot grow where taller plants such as ferns and sedges are established.

The flowers are small and yellow-green and the leaves, especially the uppermost ones which surround the flowers, are a similar colour so what is visible is a yellow-green low growing band of vegetation. The leaves are slightly fleshy which is unusual for a woodland plant and have large white hairs on them.

Apart from the arrangement of the leaves, Alternate-leaved Saxifrage has other slight differences from the Opposite-leaved Saxifrage. It grows a little taller, is slightly more robust and has a stem which is triangular in cross-section as opposed to the square cross-section of the Opposite-leaved Saxifrage. Finally, the Alternate-leaved variety is said to prefer slightly more alkaline areas. All too often when you suspect the plant you have found may be the rare Alternate-leaved species, you bend down to inspect it only to find that it is just the common species. After doing this ten or twenty times, your back starts to ache and you don't bother any more.

Surprisingly for such a small plant, it was selected as the wild flower for the county of Clackmannanshire, Scotland.

Opposite-leaved Saxifrage

Opposite-leaved Saxifrage

BUTTERBUR
Petasites hybridus

Butterbur flowers before it produces its leaves. The flower is impressive, and resembles a deconstructed cone, and it varies in colour from light pink to dark purple. There are distinct male and female flowers, which occur on different plants. Male plants are less likely to be encountered and are usually shorter with more compact florets. The individual florets become more spaced apart as the spring progresses and the flower spike increases in length. After flowering, the leaves appear and these grow large, at least 50cm across. Traditionally, these leaves were used to wrap butter to stop it melting.

One of the inevitable consequences of writing a book about woodland wild flowers is that you need to have photographs of each species. I have a large number of pictures, not all well filed. Fortunately, I also have a very good memory for photographs I have taken, and usually a recollection of the circumstance pertaining to them. I knew I had taken a photograph of Butterbur whilst on a trip to Poland some years ago and I remember it was taken in the far south east of Poland in the Bieszczady National Park, which we visited for about three days with a local guide. So, after a short search through my files, I managed to locate the photograph of the Butterbur which is a fine specimen.

In due course I wanted some more Butterbur photographs from UK woodlands but it was already late April, so a bit too late for the Butterbur flowers although the leaves were doing well. In the following year I went back at the beginning of March. The flowers were emerging at this time, but no leaves were present.

Butterbur

GREEN ALKANET
Pentaglottis sempervirens

Green Alkanet

Green Alkanet is a naturalised plant which is native to south western Europe but not Britain. Many people have this woodland plant growing in their gardens, but some evidently do not want it in there and it is quite difficult to eradicate once established.

Personally, I like the plant. The flowers are small, but they are bright blue and attractive, not dissimilar to an oversized Forget-me-not to which it is related, along with Borage and Comfrey. Why it is called Green Alkanet when it has bright blue flowers I do not know. It is favoured by insects as a source of nectar which is important early in the year.

The scientific name *Pentaglottis* means five tongues, and I assume this relates to its five petals which are vaguely tongue shaped. Its species name *sempervirens* means 'always alive' and this probably refers to the difficulty in getting rid of it once established. Its roots penetrate deeply and also snap fairly easily, so attempts to dig it up will almost inevitably leave a few bits of root behind and these will quickly regenerate.

It comes into flower in mid-April and continues to flower well into the summer. It is a plant that dislikes acidic soils, which is to say it is a calcicole. It tolerates shade and is often found in hedgerows and open woodlands, but is not averse to a bit of sunshine, so can be found colonising rough open ground as well.

WOOD ANEMONE

Anemone nemorosa

The Wood Anemones usually appear in March. They are one of the first winter flowers to appear in woodland, after Celandine. The plants grow in patches as they have a rhizome system and spread slowly through the ground, as do several woodland plants such as Dog's Mercury, so that one cannot be sure where one plant starts and another ends.

The name derives from the Greek word for wind, *anemos*, hence anemone is also known as the wind flower. Another, less glamorous name, is Smellfox, because the smell of the leaves is reminiscent of the scent of a fox.

The Wood Anemone is in the Buttercup family and has a typical Ranunculus type of flower, but it is white rather than the yellow of Buttercups and Celandines. The flower can sometimes appear slightly pink.

It flowers very soon after the first leaves make their appearance. The petals are technically called tepals as the Wood Anemone does not have separate sepals and petals, but just one set of about seven tepals which perform the dual function of protecting the reproductive parts of the flower when in bud and looking pretty and attracting pollinators when the flower opens into bloom. Most of the seeds are sterile and it generally reproduces asexually, its underground rhizomes creeping outwards and thus extending its coverage very gradually. This slow colonisation is the reason why its presence is an indicator of ancient woodlands.

Wood Anemone

However caution needs to be exercised in this regard because it is also a popular garden plant and some gardeners are inclined to throw garden refuse into a quiet spot in the countryside and thus introduce it into newly wooded areas.

As with many true woodland plants, the leaves do not stay around long. Once the trees are in leaf and the woodland floor becomes shadier, the Wood Anemone leaves turn yellow and die, as early as May.

The Romans believed that the first Anemone flower of the season should be plucked as a charm against fever. In more recent times it was gathered while saying '*I gather this against all diseases,*' and was then tied around an invalid's neck. It was used in rituals of healing or added to a bath to cure leprosy. The Anemone's connections to the legend of Adonis' demise also make it sought after in rituals of death and dying. The story goes that Adonis was gored by a wild boar during a hunting trip and died in Aphrodite's arms as she wept. His blood mingled with her tears and became the Anemone flower.

On Good Friday a couple of years ago my wife and I went for a walk in local woods and came across a lady picking a few anemones for her local church. She had them in a glass bowl and she had another bowl containing moss. Picking wild flowers for non-commercial reasons is still legal unless in a special conservation area or if they are very rare. Uprooting wild flowers is however illegal.

Wood Anemone with some Dog's Mercury leaves

MOSCHATEL

Adoxa moschatellina

Moschatel is also called Town Hall Clock because at the end of the flower stalk it has five flowers, four of which are aligned so that they point out at angles like the four faces on a clock tower. The fifth one faces upwards – so that you could read the time if you were flying over.

It is a small flower and difficult to spot. What catches the eye are creamy yellow dots against the green foliage. Sometimes they develop into a fairly dense patch but often they are loosely mixed in with other vegetation. The leaves are similar to flat-leaved parsley but each leaflet has a little point at the apex, almost like a tiny spike. It flowers in April.

This plant is another indicator of ancient woodland but it can also be found in hedgerows. Many hedgerows are in fact simply long narrow ancient woodlands. On the list of ancient woodland indicator species produced by Oliver Rackham,

this species scored 12 out of a maximum of 18 suggesting that it is a very strong indicator. However I remember that it grew at the side of a path leading into the wooded area of Foulden Common in Norfolk, a place to which I often took A-level Biology students. Indeed several students made their individual study on the distribution of woodland and non-woodland species along this path.

The point was that Foulden Common had historically been more or less all open grassland until some areas of the common developed into woodland, following the reduction in grazing which was due to a combination of myxomatosis and changes in farming methods, so the woods were only about sixty years old. Even so, at the beginning of this path there were several 'woodland' species, including Bluebell, Welsh Poppy, Ground Ivy, Bugle and a couple of patches of Moschatel. Possibly they arrived on the boots of visitors, including my students.

Moschatel

Careful examination of the Moschatel flower shows that it has five petals, sometimes only four. It has two stamens and one stigma per petal but one needs good eyes to see this - or a little hand lens.

It is sometimes said that it produces a musk-like scent in the evening, provided the leaves are not squashed or damaged, but I have never personally noticed a smell from this plant.

It is a perennial plant and has rhizomes to enable it to survive the winter and to aid its spread. It is more common in Wales and Scotland but less so in England and there are none in Ireland according to the BSBI map.

WILD DAFFODIL

Narcissus pseudonarcissus

Wild Daffodils are smaller and more delicate than many of their garden cousins. Daffodils are often seen growing in woods, but they are not necessarily wild ones and are frequently escapees from gardens. Wild Daffodils flower at the same time as the garden varieties, in early March.

Wild Daffodils have a peculiar distribution. They are fairly rare in the counties along the south coast and are found most commonly from Gloucestershire to Lancashire and throughout Wales. There is a region of East Anglia where they can also be found, and they are dotted about in various localities up into Scotland.

The corona, which is the trumpet-like part of the flower, has parallel sides and only fans out right at the tip. The leaves are flat and roughly 5-15mm wide, and usually thirty centimetres long and have a bluish tinge. The outer whorl of tepals are slightly paler than the central corona, and both are usually the same length. Tepals are usually 18-40mm long and twisted at the base.

Interestingly the shape of the daffodil flower causes an increased temperature inside the corona and as much as 8°C above the outside temperature has been recorded. This is a big advantage to small bees in cold weather. They can not only visit the flower to stock up on pollen but can also have a warm up.

Wild Daffodil

The flowers produce seeds which, when germinated, take five to seven years to produce a flowering plant. Unfortunately, the purity of the species is threatened by the planting of garden varieties, in the same way as the native bluebell is threatened by the planting of the Spanish Bluebell. It would be helpful if people living near to known populations of Wild Daffodils refrained from planting daffodils in their gardens. There are lots of other species which they could plant that flower at that time of year. Just a thought!

TOOTHWORT

Lathraea squamaria

Toothwort is an odd-looking plant. It is similar to the Broomrape but looks more fleshy and pink.

Toothwort grows throughout much of Britain and Ireland but is not common anywhere. It is absent in the Highlands of Scotland and also from the lowlands of East Anglia. It does grow in some woods near where I live, in which there is a lot of old Hazel which was perhaps once coppiced. There are also a few Alders and Beech there, all of which can be the host species for Toothwort, it being a parasitic plant. I have found it growing in amongst very young Ramsons and close to the host tree. Once the leaves of the Ramsons had developed, they would have grown above the Toothwort, making it very difficult to spot, so timing is all-important!

Toothwort is a total parasite, meaning it has to rely entirely on other plants for its energy. Many plants are partial parasites, having some chlorophyll, and thus being able to produce some of their own food. Examples of partial parasites are Mistletoe,

Red Bartsia and Yellow Rattle. Toothwort does not have leaves, but simple bracts which are much reduced to tiny appendages and are hidden between the flowers. The flowers bear a vague resemblance to teeth, hence the name. I have heard Toothwort referred to as Corpse-flower because country folk once thought that it grew from buried bodies... a bit gruesome but I can see where they are coming from.

Toothwort

WHITE DEAD NETTLE
Lamium album

White Dead Nettle is similar to Stinging Nettle and many people might be a bit wary about touching the leaves. However, the leaves are greener and softer in appearance than the Stinging Nettle. They can in fact be eaten raw and, as with Stinging Nettles, the leaves can be boiled like spinach and used in soups. I have tried Stinging Nettle soup and to be honest it was disappointing. The more ingredients that are added to it, such as chicken stock, cream, pepper and so on, the better it gets!

Once in flower, the White Dead Nettle is easily distinguished with its small but attractive blooms. They are, not surprisingly, white but they have little brown marks or lines at the back of the flower (honey guides) visible on close inspection.

The flowers are arranged in whorls each made up of about ten individual flowers which often bloom quite early in the year. I have seen them flowering as early as February but generally they flower from May and then throughout the summer. The species is common and found in a variety of habitats, not just woodland. They are often part of the hedgerow flora.

Local names include White Archangel, Helmet-flower and Adam-and-eve-in-the-bower, the latter name deriving from the fact that if the flower is turned upside down, beneath the white upper lid of the corolla, the black and gold stamens lie side by side like two human figures.

The flowers produce a significant amount of nectar but it is located well down inside the flower so only large insects with long tongues can reach it. Hence it is commonly visited by the larger bumblebees. Once pollinated, it will produce four small seeds (nutlets) per flower. There is no special dispersal mechanism. They just fall out when ripe. Underground, the plant also produces horizontally-growing rhizomes like its close relative the Stinging Nettle, but they are not quite so rampant as those of the Stinging Nettle. However, when pieces get broken off and moved then they can easily root and produce a new colony somewhere else.

White Dead Nettle

PRIMROSE

Primula vulgaris

There are lots of plants that have the species name *vulgaris* as it simply means common. The Primrose is one of four Primula species in Britain, of which two others are woodland ones: Oxlip and False Oxlip.

Primroses are the ones most likely to be seen. They flower in March and traditionally continue flowering into April although with recent milder conditions they now seem to be flowering throughout the winter months.

Oxlip

False Oxlip

Primroses have one flower per stalk and are primrose yellow. That statement is not as daft as it sounds: most people, when selecting paint for example, will know primrose yellow even if they have never seen a Primrose. Cowslips have lots of flowers per stalk, the colour is more of an apricot yellow and the individual flowers are smaller than those of the Primrose. However they don't grow in woods. Oxlips also have lots of flowers per stalk and the colour is a shade of yellow similar to that of the Primrose. The individual flowers look like small Primroses and all the flowers point in one direction. False Oxlip is a hybrid of a Primrose and a Cowslip. It looks like an Oxlip but the flowers on top of each stalk point in every direction. It is quite rare.

All the species in the Primula family have a clever way of preventing self-pollination. The flowers on each plant are either all pin-eyed or all thrum-eyed. This is known as heterostyly. Pin-eyed flowers have the stigma near the top of the petals and thrum-eyed flowers have the stamens near the

Primrose

top of the petals. The effect is that when pollinating insects visit the flowers, they transfer the pollen of the thrum-eyed flowers to the stigma of the pin-eyed flowers and vice versa. All flowers on a particular plant are of one sort.

The point of all this is that it leads to a better mix of the genes in the plant's offspring which means that they stand more chance of being able to colonise slightly less favourable areas, to fight off localised disease or to adapt to new conditions.

It helps their chances of survival.

The Primrose was selected by the people of Leeds as their flower in the 2002 nationwide Plantlife 'County Flowers' campaign.

Primrose

YELLOW STAR OF BETHLEHEM

Gagea lutea

Yellow Star of Bethlehem

Yellow Star of Bethlehem is one of those iconic species that wild flower enthusiasts just *have* to see. This little woodland plant is quite rare and it flowers particularly well in some years, and then just produces leaves for the next few years, rather like some orchids. It flowers from late March into April.

It favours a coppiced woodland on alkaline soil which is also quite wet, close to streams and rivers. It can be found in a band up through the centre of England and into southern Scotland, as well as in a small area of East Anglia.

I met up with this rarity in a small reserve in Warwickshire where permission to visit is required. This was obtained. I was fortunate to meet up with three other naturalists who were just leaving as I arrived. They had spent two hours searching for the said iconic species and luckily for me they had found some just before they left, information which they very generously shared with me. I was thus spared hours of searching – just as well as I had a wife and two grandchildren waiting in the car!

The local Wildlife Trust had marked where the individual plants were growing, which did make spotting them somewhat easier and also made it less likely that one trod on them accidentally. These little plants are fairly insignificant. Their leaves look like those of bluebells, of which there were many in the vicinity, and the flowers can be taken for Lesser Celandine from a distance.

The Yellow Star of Bethlehem is in the Lily family and related to the Martagon Lily and Wild Tulip, also species which throw wild flower enthusiasts into raptures. It has six yellow tepals, which have a hint of a slight green line running down the centre, which is only sometimes visible. Another distinguishing feature is that the leaves are folded into a hooded tip, unlike the leaves of bluebells. However the ones in the wood I visited all seemed to have the ends of their leaves nipped off. I was not sure what had caused this, possibly very low temperatures earlier in the year or maybe slugs. Most of the flower heads only had one or two flowers on and two or three stalks that ended in nothing so there were no developing seed pods.

But luckily this plant is a lily and has bulbs in the soil, so it is not fully reliant on seed production. Its starchy bulb is edible in emergencies and can be eaten boiled, dried, soaked or milled into flour. The seeds have elaiosomes (a fleshy 'cap' full of proteins) to attract ants who then distribute the seeds. It also spreads vegetatively through the small lateral bulbils that form in the axils of the bulb so with three different methods of reproduction one might think that this flower would be more common.

Ground Ivy

GROUND IVY
Glechoma hederacea

Ground Ivy

Ground Ivy is a common woodland plant although it will also grow in more open areas. It is not related to Ivy but it grows in a similar way by creeping along the ground but it will not grow up vertical surfaces such as tree trunks or walls. It is in fact part of the large *lamiaceae* family which includes all the nettles.

It has typical labiate characteristics which are stems that are square in cross section and the typical nettle flower shape which consists of a tube of five fused petals with the lower pair of petals sticking out as a lip. The flowers are a purplish blue and they appear from March or April and then keep going for several months. The flowers are fairly small but as the plant produces many, it can result in an impressive display.

The leaves are not ivy shaped. They are a rounded kidney shape and have crenellated edges. They are soft and covered with fine hairs. This plant reacts to the amount of light in which it is growing. If the light is bright then the leaves will be quite small and often develop a purple colour. This pigmentation exists to protect the photosynthetic pigments of chlorophyll which can break down if the light is too intense.

If the woodland is shady, the leaves grow much bigger and have no need to produce the purple secondary pigments. In fact, the leaves will produce more chlorophyll than normal and thus look a darker green. Another clever little trick that Ground Ivy has up its sleeve is to produce longer inter-nodal sections in dark conditions so that the distance between one pair of leaves on the stem to the next pair of leaves is much greater. If the amount of light being received is sufficient then the plant benefits from staying in that area, so keep the inter-nodal distance short and it will not inadvertently grow into a less well-lit region. If on the other hand light is a problem, then if the stem growth is longer it will be more likely to grow into an area more conducive to its well-being. The plant has the ability to produce roots at each node so as it grows it sends down new roots to establish and maintain itself. It is a bit like predators searching for prey. If there are lots of rabbits in one area then a fox does not have to travel too far to catch his dinner. If the rabbit population is low and thinly spread, then the fox has to increase his hunting range in order to get sufficient food.

Ground Ivy is a perennial and is native to Europe but has spread all over the world. I saw it growing in Ushuaia, on the southernmost tip of Argentina. It will reproduce asexually but it also produces seeds and can be spread in that way too.

If the leaves are crushed they are said to produce a pleasant smell. It can be used to make tea and there are lots of references to using it as an ingredient in salad and to its having various medicinal uses. However, it should be eaten or used sparingly as it contains various chemicals some of which may be harmful if taken in larger quantities. One interesting use for Ground Ivy is that it causes milk to set and can be used as an alternative to rennet, thereby producing cheese suitable for vegetarians.

It was also employed years ago to flavour ale before hops were extensively used. The ale mixture was called gruit and was a combination of herbs, commonly including Sweet Gale, Mugwort, Yarrow, Ground Ivy, Horehound and Heather. The decline of gruit ale was not only caused by the increase in hopped beer but also because it did not meet with the approval of the Catholic Church. It was said to be highly intoxicating and an aphrodisiac when consumed in sufficient quantity. Recently with the increase of craft beers there has been a minor recovery in the production of gruit ales.

LUNGWORT

Pulmonaria officinalis

Lungwort

Lungwort is a wild flower classed as naturalised. It is native to Europe and to the Middle East. It has flowers which start off pink and then gradually turn blue as the flower gets older. It flowers in March through to May, and is usually found in shady places such as woodlands and hedgerows.

Lungwort produces seeds in the form of nutlets so movement of seeds from place to place, via mud picked up on the feet of walkers and wild or domestic mammals is a means of transport. The nutlets are smooth, egg-shaped, brown, up to 4.5mm long and 3mm wide, each containing a single seed. Up to four nutlets per flower are produced, ripening mostly in summer.

Lungwort leaves are wide, hairy and with pale cream or white spots. There is a species, Narrow-leaved Lungwort, which is restricted in Britain to an area around Southampton, where it is native. As one would expect, this has longer

narrower leaves and the flowers are a little smaller and darker blue.

The white spots give the plant its name as they are similar in appearance to the spots on diseased lungs. The plant was once used as a medicine to prevent or cure lung disease, hence its common name and indeed its scientific name *Pulmonaria*, pulmonary relating to the lungs. However there is not much evidence that substances found in the plant have any effect, positive or negative, on the well-being of the lungs. It does have a high mucilage content which could possibly have a soothing effect on a cough and in common with a huge numbers of other plants it contains antioxidants which can be randomly beneficial. There is also a Lungwort moss which is used medicinally although it is not a moss at all but a lichen!

BILBERRY

Vaccinium myrtillus

Bilberry flowers

The Bilberry is usually associated with heath and moorland, but it is also commonly found in light woodland.

It starts to flower in early April, but its main flowering period is mid to late April. Later in the year, with luck, the blue fruits appear. These are edible and look like small Blueberries.

The Bilberry is a low-growing shrub. It can reach 50-70cm in height and is sometimes quite straggly when growing in more shaded areas.

Since 2000 Bilberry has been succumbing to a fungal infection called bilberry blight in Britain. This turns the affected part of the plant brown, so that it appears to be dead. It started in the south of England but is spreading and is now affecting an area as far north as The Roaches in the millstone grit area of the Pennines. Attempts are being made to stop it spreading.

The fruits contain various chemicals called anthocyanins which are used for improving eyesight and night vision and in delaying the onset of cataracts and other eye disorders, especially age-related macular degeneration. The anthocyanins help to regenerate rhodopsin, a purple dye involved in night vision. So all you oldies, me included, get out there and collect and eat your Bilberries.

Bilberries are the food plant of the rare Silurian Moth which is very good at seeing in the dark! I have not seen any caterpillars on the Bilberries growing in my wood but will keep an eye open for them in the future.

Records of Silurian Moths in Monmouthshire show that they have been found in the Brecon Beacons, not that far away from our wood as the moth flies.

GREATER STITCHWORT
Stellaria holostea

There is a small amount of Greater Stitchwort growing in my wood in Monmouthshire. It prefers to grow on the surrounding very old stone wall which has lots of trees and bushes growing out of it but which also supports a few wild flowers, not only Stitchwort but also Wood Sage, Wood Anemone and some Common Vetch. The wall is topped with Common Polypody fern. I suspect that the reason the

Stitchwort grows by the wall here is because the location is drier than most of the wood which can become fairly waterlogged during the winter and early spring. Such conditions are probably not to the Stitchwort's liking.

The plant is a member of the Caryophyllaceae family, commonly known as Pinks. This family includes Campions, Ragged Robin, Pinks and Stitchworts, Mouse-ears and

Greater Stitchwort

Pearlworts, to name but a few. The main characteristics of the family are that the stems often show a slight swelling at each node and attached to each node are a pair of leaves. The flowers usually have five sepals and five petals. The petals are often notched and certainly are in the case of the Greater Stitchwort.

My mother called them Shirt Buttons, and on researching it I found that Stitchwort was, indeed, known as Daddy's Shirt Buttons. It has some other common names such as Wedding Cake and, confusingly, Star of Bethlehem as there are several other plants also referred to by that name. My mother did not have a huge knowledge of wild flowers but she could put names to quite a few and often these were old-fashioned names such as Peggles for Cowslips.

As a small child I used to go to Sunday school at the local church in Galleywood in Essex. In the autumn the church held a harvest festival in which there were competitions for children which involved flowers. One such competition was for a 'floating garden' which was just a dish containing water with flowers or petals arranged artistically to float. In my small boy's mind this was definitely one for the girls! Another category was a miniature garden – but one I liked and remember my mother helping me with was the competition for the biggest and best bunch of wild flowers. I never won but I used to plunder and pillage the countryside looking for the most spectacular wild flowers I could find, thereby unknowingly doing my small bit to ensure that today we have rare and threatened species! My mother's contribution was to prepare them all and arrange them tastefully, presumably at the same time telling me the names of the ones she knew.

There is another species called Lesser Stitchwort which predictably is smaller and more delicate than the Greater Stitchwort. I have seen this growing in woodlands. It grows in grassy heathlands, often on acidic soils, but nevertheless it does also grow in woodlands.

WOOD SORREL

Oxalis acetosella

Wood Sorrel is not related to the Sorrels called Rumex which look like miniature dock plants. This sorrel is an Oxalis and has trifoliate leaves like clover, although it is not related to clover either.

Wood Sorrel grows in very shady places in the woods. There was a very small patch of it growing in my bit of Ninewells Wood, but once all the Corsican Pines were removed, I did not seen it again. Possibly the disruption caused by the felling and subsequent clearing of the brash removed this very small colony. This is why, in an ideal world, clear-felling should be avoided. However, our conifers were diseased and we could only obtain a felling licence for a clear-fell.

Wood Sorrel is one of the plants which indicates 'ancient woodland' status. The flowers are cleistogamous, which means that they undergo pollination and fertilisation before the flower opens. It is reported that Wood Sorrel rushes to bloom early in the spring before other vegetation shades it, and while it is easy for nectar-hunting insects to find the plant's large flowers. Later in the summer the plant refrains from producing large open flowers in favour of cleistogamous flowers that do not open but resemble buds.

Wood Sorrel

Even though these summer flowers are self-pollinating, the seeds usually develop well – belt and braces. The plant can also spread by rhizomes, which is why the colonies are often circular in shape.

The leaves are edible. I have sampled them and they are tangy. They contain oxalic acid, which gives them their sharp flavour. Whilst perfectly safe to eat in small quantities, the leaves should not be eaten in large amounts since oxalic acid can bind up the body's supply of calcium leading to nutritional deficiency. The quantity of oxalic acid is reduced if the leaves are cooked.

People with a tendency to rheumatism, arthritis, gout, kidney stones or hyperacidity should take especial caution if including this plant in their diet since it has been known to aggravate those conditions.

The shramrock-like leaves act as mini weather-indicators, closing before and during rainfall and at dusk.

The flowers are delicate and beautiful with fine purple lines drawing the eye to the orange-yellow centre. This design is to attract pollinating insects. It also provides those of us who like wild flowers with a little gem to appreciate. The citrus-green leaves are trifoliate and really delicate, a delightful sight in early spring.

SHEEP'S SORREL

Rumex acetosella

Sheep's Sorrel flowers are small and the plant itself does not grow very tall. Occasionally if there is a thick concentration of the plants they give a rusty red colouration to the scene, which in the early morning light can look beautiful.

The first flowers appear in March and it goes on flowering throughout the summer and into the autumn. As with all the plants in this genus, the leaves are arrow shaped. Culinary buffs will be familiar with a related species called Common Sorrel or Garden Sorrel *Rumex acetosa*, often simply called Sorrel. There is a page dedicated to it on Waitrose's website so it must be a 'foody' plant. Several years ago I planted some in my garden along with various other plants such as mint,

Sheep's Sorrel

Sheep's Sorrel

thyme and sage. All the other herbs died except for the Sorrel which has not only maintained itself but set seed and spread into other areas. I do not find it particularly useful as it is a bit too acidic and tangy for my taste. The variety I planted was a garden cultivar and as such had larger leaves. The original wild woodland species has much smaller leaves which are nonetheless still chunkier than the rather thin and often elongated leaves of Sheep's Sorrel.

Sheep's Sorrel is unisexual (dioecious) so all the flowers on one plant are either male or female. Female flowers tend to be green, male flowers yellow and the whole plant is generally reddish green to brown.

It is a perennial and has a strong and resilient root stock to carry it through the winter. Even though it is quite a small plant, the roots can extend as far as 50cm down into the ground.

It is more a heathland plant than a woodland species and definitely prefers acidic soils but I have seen it growing in several woodlands although not in the shadiest of sections. Being low growing, it does not tolerate too many taller plants so it is often seen in the more open or fringe areas of woods. It is the food plant for the caterpillar of the Small Copper butterfly.

THREE-NERVED SANDWORT

Moehringia trinervia

Three-nerved Sandwort is a small plant with little white flowers. It is hardly the most exciting plant in the world. It is low growing and often tucked in between other larger plants. However whilst one's spirit might be lifted more by seeing a Military Orchid or a Marsh Gentian, the humble Three-nerved Sandwort is still a woodland species with its own individual genetic make-up and thus must rank equally alongside all other plants.

The common Dandelion is a most beautiful plant and when a roadside bank is covered with them in early spring they make a show which rivals a field of Fritilliaries or a woodland glade bedecked with Wild Daffodils but as they are more common we might just give them the honour of pausing and admiring but are unlikely to make a special visit to photograph or paint them. I fear the Three-nerved Sandwort suffers similar neglect.

I will try to do it justice. It is called Three-nerved because

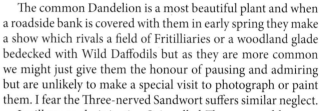

the leaves have a central vein and two major side veins running out from the leaf stalk. They are not obvious on all leaves and perhaps show up more when viewed from the underside. Occasionally they have two veins either side of the central one.

The flower has five little simple round petals. They are not notched and deeply indented like the Stitchworts and Chick weeds. The plant does look superficially like a Chickweed but the simple little oval petals distinguish Sandworts from similar plants with little white flowers. The other distinctive feature is the five sepals which are pointed and stick out between and beyond the petals. The sepals are often described as being twice as long as the petals but I have found that they vary and sometimes the sepals are only just longer than the petals.

Three-nerved Sandwort favours rich, damp forests and semi-shade and it can be found growing alone or in small patches on moss-covered rocky ledges, on boulders, crags and beside streams

Three-nerved Sandwort

– places that are too small for tree roots, and where the leaf canopy is therefore open. The upper parts of seashores where the waves have deposited debris offer the plant an open and nutritious habitat although it is no salt-lover. Sometimes it grows on open, calciferous rocks.

Three-nerved Sandwort and Common Chickweed *Stellaria media* look a lot like each other at first glance but on closer inspection a whole host of differences become apparent. Chickweed's stem is only hairy on one side, whilst Three-nerved Sandwort is short-haired all over; Chickweed's leaves are stalked and the leaf blade is feather-veined, Three-nerved Sandwort's stalks are almost non-existent and the leaf blade is clearly three-veined. More differences can be found in the small, white flowers. Chickweed's sepals are blunt and the petals are so deeply lobed that its five petals look as if there are ten. Three-nerved Sandwort's sepals are sharp and its petals are unlobed.

Three-nerved Sandwort is common throughout England and Wales but less so into Scotland, particularly as you get further north.

Lords and Ladies in autumn

LORDS AND LADIES

Arum maculatum

Lords and Ladies, Wild Arum and Cuckoo Pint are some of its common names but its scientific name is *Arum maculatum* and it flowers in April. Its common names often have sexual connotations. It is not the most beautiful flower in the world but it is large and distinctive and it is very interesting.

The leaves of this plant normally appear around the end of February. It is a plant of the edges of woodlands and the hedgerows. It is tolerant of shade but does not flourish in really dark conditions. The leaves are large and arrow-shaped and sometimes have dark purple blotches on them.

In April up pops the flower which is not like any normal flower – it is a curled up spike which narrows at the base and then becomes swollen before the stalk disappears into the ground. This peculiar rolled up pointed protuberance is called a spathe and it can vary in colour from pale yellow through to various shades of green and even purple.

This spathe eventually unrolls to reveal a club-shaped central spike which is called a spadix and this too can vary in colour from dark purple through to lemon yellow. The spadix produces a smell of ammonia and amines, a bit like urine, which attracts little flies. From here on in it all gets a bit complicated. It is the little flies which are the all-important part of this story. Having been attracted to the smelly spadix they are funnelled down towards the swollen base of the flower.

This process is aided by the shape of the spathe and its slippery surface. Where the spathe narrows before the swollen lower part, there is a ring of little hairs and these all point downwards. This allows the flies to squeeze past them but stops them getting back out. It is important to point out that these flies will have previously visited another Arum flower and will be covered with pollen from that flower so now the flies are covered with pollen from another plant and having got past the hairs, the flies are stuck in this swollen chamber at the base of the spathe. In this chamber are the female flowers, the ovules, which are at this stage receptive to pollen and so the flies inadvertently deposit pollen on the ovules. Thus the female flowers will be pollinated by pollen from another flower.

Once the female flowers are pollinated, this triggers the male flowers into action and the anthers burst open, exposing their pollen, and the poor little flies now get a fresh covering of pollen.

The plant then produces a little exudation of nectar, a small reward for the flies and a nice energy boost for the next part of their adventure.

By this stage the Lords and Ladies' ovules which were pollinated a few days ago are no longer receptive and so will not be pollinated by pollen from the anthers.

Now for the final piece in the jigsaw. Once the flies have got a new coating of pollen and have topped up their calories, the hairs at the top which they earlier squeezed past wither up and die so the flies can escape from their little prison and go on their way to the next flower and repeat the whole process.

If this rather complicated system to ensure cross-pollination works out, then the ovules develop, the spathe and spadix disappear and in the autumn one is left with a spike of red berries which look attractive but which I believe are poisonous.

No doubt the whole system works very well as this is a prolific plant.

One very occasionally comes across a similar species with attractive white veins in the leaves. This is Italian arum *Arum italicum* and it is a garden escapee.

Lords and Ladies showing spadix

CREEPING BUTTERCUP

Ranunculus repens

Creeping Buttercup is one of the four most common Buttercups found in Britain. The other three are the Meadow Buttercup which is found more often, not surprisingly, in meadows, the Bulbous Buttercup, also found in more open spaces, and the Goldilocks Buttercup – *see page 58* – which is a purely woodland species. There are other less common species such as the Corn Buttercup, Small-flowered Buttercup, Hairy Buttercup and Celery-leaved Buttercup.

The main characteristic of the Creeping Buttercup is that it produces runners or stolons like a strawberry and it can in that way spread and colonise a wider and wider area.

The stolons are often just below the ground, unlike those of strawberries, and in the woods and countryside they are a very welcome addition to our flora.

The flowers of Buttercups are regarded by botanists as being primitive. There are several reasons for this. First of all the various parts are all attached separately so each petal and each sepal is a separate entity, in contrast to the tubular flowers of something like a foxglove.

Secondly the numbers of each part can vary. Creeping Buttercups usually have five petals per flower but there could be as many as eight. The same variation in numbers applies to other parts such as the stamens and carpels. The stamens and

Creeping Buttercup

carpels are arranged in a spiral. This is difficult to see from a casual glance but were one to examine a flower carefully, perhaps with the aid of a binocular microscope, then this would become apparent. This spiral arrangement is also found in magnolias and is regarded as more primitive because it is the same arrangement as in pine cones and conifers, which are less advanced than the flowering plants.

If one finds a Buttercup flower with six, seven or even eight petals, then generally all flowers in that area will be the same because all the plants will be genetically identical, having developed by the spread of the stolons.

To tell the Buttercups from one another, one has to look at the leaves. They are all complex, that is to say made up of lots of leaflets but in the Creeping Buttercup and the Bulbous Buttercup these are separate and do not link one leaflet to another, so a Buttercup where the leaf is entire must be a Meadow Buttercup. Another characteristic of the Meadow Buttercup is its height: it can grow tall, to over a metre.

To distinguish Creeping Buttercup from Bulbous Buttercup, the former obviously creeps and has stolons. The Bulbous Buttercup has a swollen bulb at its base but one should not really go digging them up to check if it has a bulb or not. The easy way, if it is flowering, is to look at the sepals. If they curve back along the stem it is a Bulbous Buttercup. If they stick out and curve up underneath the petals, then it is Creeping Buttercup. In addition the flower stem of the Creeping Buttercup is grooved, unlike that of the Meadow Buttercup which also has its sepals curved up in the same way as the Creeping Buttercup.

The name Ranunculus derives from Rana which is the scientific name for frog so it means 'little frog'. Possibly the name was given to buttercups because they often grow in damp places where you might find a frog, but that explanation seems a bit tenuous.

Most of the Ranunculus family are poisonous. Buttercups are poisonous, but not as much as some of the other members of the group such as Monkshood and Aconites.

There is research which suggests that there is a link between the occurrence of Creeping Buttercup flowers with above the normal number of five petals to the age of the grassland.

This research found that each plant of Creeping Buttercup in an area with flowers that had additional petals in a sample of 100 was found to equate to approximately seven years in age of the field since it was first planted or allowed to become fallow.

Early Purple Orchid

EARLY PURPLE ORCHID

Orchis mascula

The Early Purple Orchid is one of the most common British orchids. Twayblade is also very common, as is Common Spotted Orchid. Early Purple Orchids are spectacular and, unsurprisingly, purple in colour, though the depth of purple can vary and apparently some are white although I have never seen a white one. They flower at the same time as the Bluebells in or around the end of April, and they are the earliest of the Orchids to come into bloom.

The leaves usually have large purple, sometimes almost black, spots on them but this is not inevitable nor is that feature exclusively restricted to the Early Purple Orchid. Several other species, such as the Marsh Orchid and the Spotted Orchid, may have such spots.

This orchid will grow in a range of different light conditions, sometimes on the edge of woodland thereby receiving more light than others which are more centrally located. It will grow on a variety of neutral and calcareous soils, and is most frequently found in woodland, coppices and calcareous grassland. It will also grow in hedgerows, scrub, on roadsides and railway banks and on limestone pavement and moist cliff ledges. It will grow in most levels of light and favours damp soils but can be found in quite a range of soils, some of which may be quite low in water content. It shows the same adaptability with regard to pH. It prefers pH 7 but will be found growing in soils which vary from slighly acidic to quite strongly alkaline. It will even tolerate some degree of salt, so in these respects it is quite remarkable for an orchid.

Most orchids are fussy but the Early Purple Orchid's tolerance is the reason it is common. It can grow tall and has an impressive flower spike, and the derivation of the name mascula could be from the shape of its tuberous root which evidently resembles a pair of testicles. I have never dug one up and never will, as apart from being illegal, it is simply not right to interfere with wild flowers.

In some regions the roots have been used as a food source. It contains a starchy material which can be made into a type of flour called Salep. Salep flour is consumed in beverages and desserts, especially in places that were formerly part of the Ottoman Empire. An increase in consumption is causing local extinction of orchids in parts of Turkey and Iran. Salep is a traditional winter beverage in Turkey. It is sometimes served with iced coffee at certain coffee shops in Istanbul. It is claimed that Salep has aphrodisiac properties and, given the shape of the tubers from which it is made, the easy connotation is not surprising.

The flowers initially smell of honey but once they have been pollinated, the smell becomes more like that of cat urine. Pollination is carried out by insects with a long proboscis as the flowers have a fairly long spur which projects back and up from each individual flower.

Early Purple Orchid showing spotted leaves

The native Bluebell

BLUEBELL
Hyacinthoides non-scripta

Bluebells are probably the most spectacular of our woodland plants, although Wild Daffodils and Ramsons also pack quite a punch. Bluebell woods are notoriously difficult to photograph as for some reason it is very difficult to capture the blueness. They often look more purple in a photographic image.

Bluebells first appear in March, but the main show does not occur until mid to late April. In my wood, which is located at some altitude, it is even later.

There is an invasive related species, the Spanish Bluebell, which I think is not nearly as attractive. Its flowers are bigger and chunkier and the colour resembles that of a watered-down hyacinth. Many people have this species in their gardens. The native bluebell is more delicate. The flowers are all held on one side of the stem and the flower head normally droops delicately. The Spanish species is upright and much less subtle.

Unfortunately the two species hybridise so the purity of our native species is getting diluted.

Once the flowering is over the plants produce seeds and then die off. In midsummer there is very little evidence of the Bluebells. The leaves have turned white and shrivelled up and all that is visible is the flower stalks and the white seed heads containing the black seeds.

One occasionally can find white bluebells.

Unlike many woodland flowers, Bluebells have a scent. It is similar to that of hyacinths but not as powerful. They are pollinated by bees and hoverflies. Some bees cut a hole in the back of the flower to get at the nectar but because the bell is composed of individual petals closely pressed together and not actually fused as in flowers like Foxgloves, some of the more powerful bumblebees can force their tongue between the petals and gain access to the nectar via the back door.

Bluebells are one of the indicator species of ancient woodland (*see page 246*), although it is not one of the key indicator species, probably because it gets introduced into modern woodlands in order to prettify them.

In 2002 when *Plantlife* ran a 'County Flowers' campaign to assign flowers to each of the counties and metropolitan areas of the United Kingdom, surprisingly not a single county in the whole of Britain chose this beautiful and much photographed flower as its representative.

The invasive Spanish Bluebell

AMERICAN SKUNK CABBAGE

Lysichiton americanus

I recently came across some American Skunk Cabbage growing in Britain, and if anything it looked slightly bigger and lusher than that which I had seen in Canada. Where I saw it in Britain, the vegetation was mostly a tangle of Hazel, overcrowded Conifers and small Oaks.

I saw it growing in a narrow wooded valley where there was a small stream tumbling down and little waterfalls running over moss-covered boulders. There were some spectacular houses in the vicinity with the stream running down through the properties. Over the years some owners had put in dams and created little pools and lakes which is all very nice and no doubt great for the wildlife. One or two had planted some exotic plants, such as Greater Butterbur, Winter Heliotrope and Indian Rhubarb *Gunnera manicata* and a couple of them had some Skunk Cabbage in their gardens.

It is now spreading and it is no longer restricted to the

American Skunk Cabbage

areas where it was first planted. People cannot be prevented from planting exotic species in their gardens but maybe if they were made more aware of the damage they can do then they might think twice.

Skunk Cabbage is now fairly well established in many locations throughout Britain particularly in the south. I am somewhat surprised that people would want to plant Skunk Cabbage in their gardens. The clue is in the name and its smell is quite strong and not very pleasant.

Some varieties sold by garden centres in Britain do not smell so much but the ones I came across did smell a lot. I parked my vehicle a little way up from where they were growing because the road is narrow in places and when I opened the door to walk down and take some photographs I could immediately smell the plants. The smell is there to attract flies for pollination, rather like Lords and Ladies to which it is related.

In Canada the smell attracts the bears and they eat it. I remember seeing lots of warnings throughout our trip to British Columbia, not just about bears but also wolves, coyotes and cougars or mountain lions. One warning said to look out for Skunk Cabbage and if it had been eaten then probably bears were in the vicinity. We did see plenty of bears, both brown bears and grizzly bears but they seemed to be more interested in eating Dandelion flowers at that time of year.

The Skunk Cabbage has a remarkable ability to produce heat. All living things will produce some heat. This is a by-product of any metabolic process so if it snows when Crocus plants are in bloom, then the snow will always melt first around the flower, leaving the flower sticking out of a little hole in the snow.

Skunk Cabbage takes this to extremes. It can produce temperatures of between 15–35 °C (27–63 °F) above air temperature, very useful for melting a hole in Canadian snow! Some think that this increased temperature may also help to spread the foul smell thereby attracting more pollinating insects.

The spadix (the upright part at the centre of the cowl) is made up of individual units. These are all petal-less flowers, so it is different to the spadix of its relative, Lords and Ladies. Lords and Ladies' flowers are below the spadix and contained in the swollen region below the cowl so pollination in the case of Skunk Cabbage is a less complicated and more random procedure although that does not necessarily make it less efficient.

The seed pod of the American Skunk Cabbage is also quite different to the red berries of Lords and Ladies. I have not personally seen the fruit or berries of the Skunk Cabbage but it is apparently a knobbly green structure with little red bumps on each fruit. I suspect that seed production is not very common in woods in Britain.

GOLDILOCKS BUTTERCUP

Ranunculus auricomus

The Goldilocks Buttercup is very small and the flowers are not always easy to spot. Sometimes the petals are rudimentary. The leaves are not like Buttercup leaves: the upper leaves are narrow and stellate, bearing more of a resemblance to Woodruff or even Cleavers. A detailed inspection reveals a confusion of palmately lobed basal leaves along with the narrow lanceolate stem leaves on the same plant.

The distribution of this plant is patchy. It does not occur at all in quite large areas of Britain, whilst in other regions it is quite common.

It is found along the border between Wales and England but is more or less absent either side. There is a population in Suffolk and Cambridgeshire and I recall having come across it in Norfolk. The Goldilocks Buttercup is regularly found in central Scotland. It is not coastal, nor is its diverse distribution related to climate.

Goldilocks showing basal leaves

Goldilocks showing upper lanceolate leaves

FLY ORCHID
Ophrys insectifera

I have seen Fly Orchids on very rare occasions and only once in Britain. They are fairly rare and particularly so in East Anglia, so having spent most of my life in Norfolk, it was not something I was likely to bump into. In addition they are quite difficult to spot as they are small and insignificant.

The main locations of these plants are the chalk and limestone regions of England, that is to say the North and South Downs, the Chilterns and the Cotswolds. The particular specimen in the photograph was growing just outside the Cotswold area so a little beyond its normal range.

The flowers resemble insects and the method of pollination is dependant on their attraction to male digger wasps, which mistake the flowers for female digger wasps. To increase its attraction, it also produces pheromones similar to those produced by female wasps. The main species of digger wasp the Fly Orchid is trying to seduce is *Argogorytes mystaceus*.

In trying to copulate with the orchid flower, the modified stamens called pollinia (which most orchids have) get detached from the flower and stick to the wasp's head. Not having learnt its lesson and now even more desperate to meet a lady wasp, the frustrated male then finds another flower and the pollinia which contain the pollen get pushed against the stigmatic surface of the flower and so cross pollination is effected. Clever though this all is, it is not very efficient in this species of orchid and less than 20% of the flowers produce seed. This may well be one of the reasons for its rarity.

Fly Orchids flower from late April to early June and as they prefer alkaline soils, they are usually found in open deciduous woodland, particularly Beech woods. This was exactly the habitat in which I saw my one and only British individual. It was growing close to some impressive spikes of Early Purple Orchid, Bluebells and Herb Paris. Despite the competition it was the star of the show for me. I have returned to the exact same spot in subsequent years but not seen the Fly Orchid. It may still be there but just not flowering, it may have died or maybe I am just not seeing it.

Fly Orchid

BUGLE

Ajuga reptans

Bugle

Bugle showing purple upper leaves

This photograph is a splendid example of Bugle. It is shade tolerant and so is often found in woodlands, particularly the glades and at the edges of paths or alongside woodland walls. In shady positions it will often grow a bit taller, to catch the light.

It is a member of the Nettle family, the flowers having the typical lip which splits into two lobes. The stem is also square in cross section. Rather unusually, the stem has hairs on two of the sides but none on the other two sides. The leaves are shiny and often have a purplish blush. Lower down the stem, the leaves normally have an irregular or wavy edge but further up the stem the leaves become more rounded, with a smooth edge. They are almost bract-like and the purple coloration adds to the overall attraction level for visiting pollinators.

The flowers are borne in whorls at each node and usually number about eight at each junction. The structure is very similar to that of the White Dead Nettle but they do not all flower at the same time. Some Bugle will be in full bloom while others are still in bud. This is probably a form of insurance policy so that at least some will be in bloom when conditions are optimum for pollination.

It flowers between April and July and is attractive to a variety of insects including several species of Fritillary Butterfly, Green-veined Whites, Silver Y Moths, White-tailed Bumblebees and Common Carder Bees.

WOOD FORGET-ME-NOT

Myosotis sylvatica

Wood Forget-me-nots and those grown in many gardens are the same plant, so some Forget-me-nots growing in the woods may well be derived from plants that were once growing in a nearby garden.

Forget-me-nots are described as short-lived perennials (which seems a bit of a contradiction in terms) or as biennials which will survive more than two years!

They are beautiful flowers: small with bright blue petals with a yellow 'eye'. They flower in April and May. There are also white and even pink versions, no doubt coming from recent garden escapes.

There are other species of Forget-me-not, about 60 native to Europe. I have one such growing in my garden. It is *Myosotis arvensis* or the Field Forget-me-not. The flowers are much smaller and paler blue. The seed capsules stick to clothes thus effecting distribution.

This one seems to die off after flowering so appears to be more of an annual.

Forget-me-nots are the food plant of a moth called the Setaceous Hebrew Character, a brown moth which has a white mark on its fore wing which evidently looks something like a letter in the Hebrew alphabet.

There are several stories about the origin of the name which prevails in many European languages and was popular with the Victorians who enjoyed a craze for the 'language of flowers'.

The Forget-me-not is the symbol of the 1915 Armenian Genocide Remembrance and also the emblem of the International Missing Children's Day.

Wood Forget-me-not

CUCKOOFLOWER

Cardamine pratensis

I remember Cuckooflowers from my childhood although we called them Milkmaids, probably courtesy of my mother. They grew in a damp meadow surrounding a pond near my family home in Beehive Lane in the village of Galleywood, Essex. This pond was shallow and it would dry up in the summer. At some stage before we moved away from this little Essex village the pond was filled in and a house was built on the plot.

I have included this plant as a woodland wild flower because it will sometimes grow in wet woodlands provided it

Cuckooflower

is not too shady. There was quite a lot of it growing in a wood I often visited called Honeypot Wood, a coppiced woodland in Norfolk.

The Cuckooflower may derive its common name from the fact that it comes into flower at just about the same time as the first cuckoo's call is heard. Another name for it is Lady's Smock or Milkmaids. A possible source put forward for the name Milkmaids is that the flowers appear at the same time of year as the cows were put out into the meadows after a winter indoors. There are several other suggestions, some of them lewd: strange for such a delicate-looking plant!

Cuckooflower is the food plant of the Orange Tip butterfly, aptly named because the male of this member of the 'white' butterfly family *Pieridae* has orange tips to its wings. The female does not, and from above it looks quite similar to the Small white and the Green-veined white. The defining characteristic of this species is the underside of the wings which are mottled green and white and this makes a perfect camouflage against the flower heads of Cow Parsley on which the adult butterflies also often feed.

These are clever little butterflies because they only lay one egg on each Cuckooflower food plant. It was thought they had a quick check round to make sure that there were no other eggs already attached to the plant and only then would they lay the single egg. Recent studies however have established that to prevent other females from laying eggs on the same flower head, females will deposit a pheromone during egg laying. This pheromone is designed to deter other females from laying another egg on that flower head. Flower heads with more than one egg can still be found, as the pheromone is water-soluble and relatively short-lived but generally only one bright orange egg per plant will be found and this ensures that when the caterpillar hatches out, there will be sufficient food for it to grow to full size before turning into a chrysalis.

This is quite a sensible arrangement because Cuckooflowers do not grow as dense clumps as do for example Stinging Nettles, so if there were several caterpillars on one Cuckooflower plant they would at some stage run out of leaves and have to decamp to a fresh plant. With the plants growing dotted about this could prove difficult. Garlic mustard is also a food plant for the caterpillar.

Midges also live on Cuckooflowers and they cause galls to develop on the plant. If one of these galls is cut open carefully it will reveal some little grubs inside which are the larvae of the gall midge *Dasineura cardaminis*.

In 2002 when counties selected flowers to represent them, Cuckooflower was chosen by two counties as their preferred option and they were Cheshire and Breconshire.

Orange-tip butterfly egg laid on Cuckooflower

Cuckooflowers

BUSH VETCH

Vicia sepium

Bush vetch

Showing dark purple flowers in bud

Bush Vetch is easily missed but is actually quite common. It grows on the fringes of woodlands, in hedge banks and in other shady places.

It grows virtually all over Britain, perhaps less so in East Anglia. It prefers neutral to alkaline soils but it is not all that fussy. According to the BSBI *Atlas of Wild Flowers* it is to be found in 2,615 out of 2,810 of the ten kilometre squares known as hectads into which Britain is divided. Each hectad is subdivided into two kilometre squares called tetrads and recently plants have even been ascribed to one kilometre squares called monads.

It produces a small group of 5-10 individual flowers which are bunched together and this distinguishes it from other similar coloured vetches. The shade of the purple flower is variable, sometimes a darker shade, especially when the flowers have just come into bloom. The leaves are compound which is typical of the vetch family and whilst they do have tendrils on the ends, these are not very curly or extensive.

Common Vetch normally has only two or three flowers which are usually more brightly coloured. Tufted Vetch produces a much more impressive group of about twenty flowers in a long spike formation and they are a much darker purple. Wood Vetch, which is much less common, has flowers which are very pale purple, almost white, and the individual flowers are much bigger.

Bush Vetch flowers from April right through to November, so there is plenty of time to spot it.

RAMSONS

Allium ursinum

Ramsons

Ramsons, also known as Wild Garlic, smell of garlic and onions. They have white flowers and in some areas replace Bluebells as the dominant woodland wild flower so that in spring the field layer of the woods is white not blue.

Ramsons are a relative of chives and not so closely related to garlic. The scientific name, *Allium ursinum,* is a reference to bears (ursus) which are quite partial to the bulbs and will dig them up in order to eat them, as do wild boar. The Forest of Dean, where I live, is populated with wild boar, and as a result Ramsons are more scarce, whereas the Wye Valley nearby has prolific Ramsons and wild boar are less often encountered.

The flower has tepals, not separate sepals and petals. It has six of them and they form a star-like arrangement. The plant is fertile and produces seeds as the main means of propagation so it spreads more quickly than some woodland species.

Wild Garlic is widespread across most of Europe. It grows in deciduous woodlands with moist soils, preferring slightly acidic conditions. In Britain, colonies are frequently associated with Bluebells, especially in ancient woodland. It is considered to be an ancient woodland indicator species.

The plant is edible and can be used in soups. Boil some potatoes and a generous bunch of Ramson leaves in chicken stock, and blend. A thick tasty soup is the result. It has been used in Switzerland to feed cattle thereby obtaining a garlic-flavoured milk for a tasty butter. Presumably that milk would not be so good on cornflakes or in coffee!

FALSE OXLIP

Primula x polyantha

T his is a hybrid of the Cowslip and the Primrose which occurs naturally and produces a plant which looks like the very rare Oxlip.

False Oxlip flowers are borne several to a stalk, like the Cowslip, but the individual flowers are much bigger than those of a Cowslip and are almost the size of Primrose flowers. However, False Oxlips have a darker mark towards the flower centre which neither the Primrose nor the true Oxlip has.

False Oxlips flower a little later in the year than Primroses, normally in late April into May and they favour shady wooded areas.

In the true Oxlip the individual flowers are all carried to one side of the main stem, whereas in the False Oxlip they form a random bunch pointing in all directions.

The true Oxlip is very rare and not found much outside East Anglia; even there it is scare. It was chosen as the representative flower of the county of Suffolk, reflecting its rarity and the area it is most likely to be encountered. I have only seen it growing in Poland. There is a photo of the true Oxlip on page 32 for comparison.

False oxlip

False oxlip

WILD TULIP
Tulipa sylvestris

Dyrham, a stunning National Trust property near Bath, is famous for its spring displays of beautiful cultivated Tulips which are very impressive but I was there for the Wild Tulip. This is yellow and relatively small, although the flower seems to be a little too large for the stalk, so it tends to bow over, unlike the bold and erect garden varieties.

It was lucky that I bumped into the Head Gardener during my visit, as he was kind enough to show me exactly where the small colony of Wild Tulips was located.

There were about 25 plants in flower and most were just going over. Had I visited a few days later I would have struggled to find any in good condition. The best time to see them is probably around the second week in April, but obviously this will vary from year to year depending on the weather.

Wild Tulips are only found in a few locations in Britain although they probably exist as specimens in many people's gardens. The centre of their natural range seems to be the borders and lowlands of Scotland, East Anglia and there are a few other locations in the south of England where they can be found.

The tulip was in cultivation in Britain by 1596 and was recorded from the wild by 1790. It seems that it was widely naturalised by the late eighteenth and nineteenth centuries but had declined dramatically by the time the 1962 BSBI Atlas was published.

Worldwide, the Wild Tulip has an extensive range, from Portugal in Western Europe across to China and south into North Africa.

The flower is delicate and apparently has a delightful scent. The day I visited the park, it was quite windy and there were not vast numbers of Wild Tulip. Those I saw were a rich yellow colour, with petals which are pointed and curl back on themselves, rather like the Martagon Lily.

The Wild Tulip is also referred to as the Wood Tulip and it seems to prefer light woodland shade.

Wild Tulip among Cow Parsley leaves

PINK PURSLANE

Claytonia sibirica

Pink purslane

I found Pink Purslane on a wooded path near the River Usk in Monmouthshire, just five-minutes walk from where I had parked my vehicle. There were only about ten little patches of the plant and most were growing right beside the riverbank. It was a shady area with some big Ash trees above. A few weeks later, I came across some more in Scotland near Loch Lomond.

The plant is related to another species called Spring Beauty, which I have seen on sand dunes. Both plants have characteristic upper leaves which surround the small group of flowers. In the case of Pink Purslane there are two distinct leaves which wrap around and cup the flowers.

Pink Purslane is an introduced species originating from North America, particularly the west coast of Canada, and the east coast of Asia across the Pacific rim. Spring Beauty also comes from America but further south, in California. Pink Purslane was first introduced into Britain in the eighteenth century and has become established in British woodlands and countryside. Some garden specimens have recently been bred with much smaller leaves, so if specimens with that characteristic are found in the wild, they will be the result of more recent garden escapes.

It probably spreads by dropping its seeds into watercourses which float downstream to colonise suitable ground lower down. On my visit to the River Usk, I only found them growing in one short stretch.

It flowers from April to July. The flowers are pink with attractive darker pink veins. The anthers are also pink and the pollen is usually yellow.

This plant is supposed to be edible in salads. Something had been nibbling at the petals of the ones I photographed but it was not me! It is claimed that Pink Purslane is high in Omega 3 oils which are normally found in fish and algae, and it contains a host of vitamins and minerals.

BITTER VETCHLING

Lathyrus linifolius

Bitter vetchling

Bitter Vetchling is really a pea rather than a vetch, which is why its scientific name is *Lathyrus* and not *Vicia*. It is sometimes referred to as a Heath Pea and it actually looks more like a pea in that the flower is more rounded and not as elongated as vetches. The flower head only has a small number of individual flowers (4-5 is usual) whereas some of the vetches often have a lot more. The leaf has a wing-like margin along the petiole which is another characteristic more typical of the pea.

The flower is initially deep purple but it fades with time and becomes more blue. The five sepals are fused together into a little tube resembling a night cap and they are a very dark purple or blue. The typical pea flower has an upright petal known as the banner and is slightly lighter in colour. If one looks carefully, slightly darker purple veins can be seen on the Bitter Vetchling flower.

The leaf shows the winged edge, the stems are angular and also edged with a narrow wing. The leaf does not have a tendril. This species produces a rudimentary spine at the end of its compound leaf.

It is found widely in open woodlands, heathy meadows, lightly grazed pastures, and grassy banks as well as on stream banks and rock ledges in the uplands. However it is not common in East Anglia nor east of the Midlands.

GARLIC MUSTARD

Alliaria petiolata

Early season flower head

G arlic Mustard is more a hedgerow plant than a true woodland species. As its name implies, it smells of garlic, easily detected if a leaf is picked and crushed in one's hand. It was used in the past as a pot herb and possibly still is. It has several alternative and regional names, perhaps the most well-known being Jack by the hedge. Other common names include Garlic root, Hedge garlic, Sauce-alone, Jack-in-the-bush, Penny hedge and Poor man's mustard.

The photograph above was taken in April. Later in the year, as the season progresses, the flower develops into a long spike. The early leaves are heart-shaped and those produced later in the year become more triangular and pointed.

It is a member of the cabbage family Cruciferae, and has four petals which form a cross shape. This species has white petals. All parts are edible: the flavour is that of garlic, with a mustard peppery element to it. There are lots of references to the different ways in which it can be used, including chopping the leaves and adding them in a sandwich or a salad, as a pesto or in sauces for salt fish. The young leaves seem to be preferable and plants growing in woodlands would be ideal, as they are far from exhaust fumes. Garlic Mustard is sometimes spoilt by the Hairy Shieldbug, *Dolycoris baccarum*, a common insect, found on a range of low-growing plants, including White Dead Nettle and Verbascum. The adults overwinter in leaf litter or tucked into dead leaves, remaining on the plant during the winter. This is one of the worst bugs for producing a bad smell. It really loves berries, especially honeysuckle and raspberries, as it walks over them it leaves behind an awful stinking substance, making the berries inedible.

The caterpillar of the Orange Tip butterfly feeds on Garlic Mustard as well as on the Cuckooflower.

Garlic Mustard later in the season

YELLOW ARCHANGEL

Lamiastrum galeobdolon

Yellow Archangel

Yellow Archangel is one of the classic woodland wild flowers. It is very much associated with ancient woodland sites. I have some growing in my wood but unfortunately it has variegated leaves and is therefore almost certainly an escapee from a local garden. In fact I suspect that it was planted there, as a previous resident of one of the nearby cottages had a penchant for 'beautifying' the woods by planting Spanish Bluebells, Aquilegia, Forsythia and Daffodils there. I have more or less eliminated the Spanish Bluebells and the Forsythia but have yet to get to grips with the others. The variegated form is very invasive and difficult to eradicate once established.

There are various wild flowers which if found in woodland point to it being an ancient woodland – *see page 246.* Yellow Archangel is considered a fairly high indicator of ancient woodland status, as long as it is not variegated!

Yellow Archangel is a member of the nettle family and has yellow flowers which are very similar in structure to those of White Dead Nettle. All of the Nettle family have stems which are square in cross-section. The flowers have a little bit of orange in them and they look attractive at close quarters, although small. The orange lines are called honey guides and many flowers have these lines or spots on them to direct pollinating insects to the source of the nectar.

HERB ROBERT

Geranium robertianum

Herb Robert is a species of Geranium. Many people think that Geraniums are confined to the red flowers that the Swiss grow in window boxes but these are actually Pelargoniums, not Geraniums. There are many species of Geranium which grow wild in Britain, mostly Cranesbills, which vary in size and colour from Meadow Cranesbill which has large blue flowers through to the Small Flowered Cranesbill which has small, light pink flowers. There are two species of Geranium which are not Cranesbill: one of these is Herb Robert, the other is Little Robin.

Herb Robert will grow in a variety of habitats and is shade tolerant and a true woodland plant. It is not too happy in really acidic situations. It is normally pink but occasionally white.

When growing in more sunny, open woodland, the leaves often develop a red colour. Quite a few woodland plants show this characteristic. They are developing a secondary pigment which helps prevent photo oxidation of the main pigments of chlorophyll a and chlorophyll b. Whilst their job is to absorb light and use the energy to effect photosynthesis, they are damaged by too much light and their delicate chemical structure can break down. Hence the need for secondary pigments to protect them.

When the flower is over, a seed capsule develops which has a long, pointed section and a bulbous base. The seeds are contained in the base. Many Cranesbills spread their seeds by flinging them out with the help of the flexible outer wall of the tips of their carpels. Herb Robert, on the other hand, relies on two white bristles which are deeply lobed at the tip and which reveal themselves only when the tip breaks away. These fibres easily attach to passing people and animals and can thus travel long distances. If they can't find a suitable ride, the seeds attach to the plant's own leaves and stem, until the rotten carpel wall breaks and the seed falls to the ground.

Herb Robert is widely distributed throughout Britain and is very common. It flowers for a long period, almost throughout the year, but certainly from March to October.

Freshly picked leaves have a peculiar odour resembling burning tyres when crushed, and on the skin, the smell is said to repel mosquitoes. It is also associated with alternative medicine to prevent cancer.

Herb Robert

Herb Robert with leaves showing red colouration

YELLOW PIMPERNEL

Lysimachia nemorum

Yellow Pimpernel is yellow, small and similar to Creeping Jenny. It flowers early in the year, from mid-April onwards but then continues through the summer and well into September.

It is a low creeping perennial and will tolerate light shade. It is often found at the edge of woodland paths, where the vegetation is not too high, enabling it to survive. Often the petals show the aftermath of the attentions of some woodland herbivores, usually slugs or snails.

Yellow Pimpernel could be confused with Creeping Jenny *Lysimachia nummularia* which is in the same genus but has flowers which are larger and more cup-shaped.

The petals of Yellow Pimpernel show a distinct gap between each one when the flower is fully open, although the flowers often close in dull and cold conditions.

Yellow Pimpernel

Flowers showing damage from slugs

Loddon Lilies in a Sussex wood

LODDON LILY

Leucojum aestivum

The Loddon Lily is also known as the Summer Snowflake and it grows in woodlands across Britain, including the Loddon Valley. It resembles a giant Snowdrop and there are two subspecies.

The Loddon Lily and its subspecies *pulchellum* look similar and are often confused. Both grow readily in suitable situations and appear to be on the increase.

The native Loddon Lily has a main flower stalk with little teeth making a serrated edge. One needs to look carefully to see this.

I have seen this plant in an isolated woodland near Hastings in Sussex. Here it may well have been a true native, in that where it was growing was a long way from any roads or habitation and the wood was surrounded by private land, fields and other woods. Reference to the BSBI website distribution maps shows that the Loddon Lily has not been previously recorded in the hectad where I saw it but has been recorded in two adjacent hectads, one to the north and one to the west.

There are normally three or four flowers hanging down from the end of the main stalk (scape) and this is in effect an umbel but it is unlike the typical umbels of Cow Parsley and Hogweed. The Loddon Lilies flower in April, much later than Snowdrops, but despite their common names of Summer Snowflake or Summer Snowdrop, they are early spring flowers and could hardly be considered a summer flower.

After flowering, the seed pod develops into a large round structure which is spongy and can float. This may aid in the dispersal of the plants, as they often grow by water courses and the seed pods which fall into the water can be washed some distance from the parent plant. The ones I found near Hastings were in woodland next to a wet area that had a small stream running through it, which could be how these flowers arrived.

It is the county flower of Berkshire, an obvious choice since the River Loddon flows through Berkshire to meet the Thames.

Columbine

LATE SPRING
(APRIL AND MAY)

Whilst there are still flowers to be found deep in the woods in late spring, this is the time when the flowers of the open woodland glades, the woodland margins and the hedgerows come to the fore.

These plants are still shade tolerant but have not got what it takes to live in the darkest areas. Now we see a mix of biennials and perennials, unlike the species which flower earlier in the year which are almost without exception perennials.

These terms are somewhat loose. A true biennial lives for two years. In year one it grows, produces leaves, and stores food. In year two it uses the stored food to produce a tall stem topped with an array of flowers and some leaves. These leaves help the flower produce seeds which are then dispersed and, with the job done, the plant dies. However, sometimes the plant dies back and stores some food and the following year it might flower again, maybe not as luxuriantly as in the previous year but it is still alive and it could even go on for a couple more years.

By this time of year the trees and bushes are leafing up so, despite brighter skies and longer days, some parts of the woods are getting darker, so plants that can climb and scramble over others are part of this late spring scene. Cleavers and Bryonies are part of the cohort, along with a delicate little plant called Climbing Corydalis which, despite its fragile demeanour, can still seek out the brighter spots to seek an existence.

COW PARSLEY

Anthriscus sylvestris

Cow Parsley is a hedgerow species more than a true woodland plant. It definitely prefers lightly shady areas over dense woodland shade. In May the hedgerows are often completely dominated by this plant producing a frothy, bubbly border of white lines to the country lanes. Later in the year other similar species such as Hogweed, Ground Elder, Hedge Parsley, Corn Parsley and others will make an appearance and without careful observation they could all be mistaken for Cow Parsley.

Cow Parsley is the species of *Umbellifer* most people are familiar with although possibly Hogweed would run it a close second. *Umbellifers* are plants in which the little flowers are arranged into an umbel, an umbrella-like formation. In some this is almost flat and in others it curves down slightly, even more like an umbrella. The purpose of this is to make a good display to attract more pollinating insects. It makes for a convenient landing pad for them, and once the pollinators have alighted they can then crawl around and visit lots of flowers thus distributing the pollen from one flower to another. The downside is that all the flowers in one umbel are genetically identical, so a good mix of genetic material will not be achieved unless the flowers are self-sterile.

A frequent visitor to Cow Parsley flowers is the Orange Tip butterfly. When at rest with its wings closed it is superbly camouflaged, having a green and white spotty appearance which looks exactly like the flower heads. When the wings are open it is white and in the case of the males there is a distinctive Orange Tip colouration. Orange Tips only visit

Cow Parsley

Cow Parsley for the nectar. Their food plants are Hedge Garlic and Cuckooflower.

The name Cow Parsley probably has nothing to do with cows. The word 'cow' was often used in days gone by to mean 'false' so it is False Parsley because the leaves do resemble those of Parsley especially early in the year before the big flowering stem has developed. The plant could be mistaken for Parsley by its appearance, but not by its smell if crushed.

I remember that when I was a small boy we used to use the stems of Cow Parsley to make pea shooters. The technique was quite straightforward. We simply cut a stem just above the first node and then again just below the second node. This produced a hollow tube. At the time I was unfamiliar with the terms node and internode. To me they were just the joints along the stem. If we could find a stem where the distance between one node and the next was long, then so much the better. For peas we used the flower buds of May or Hawthorn before the flowers opened in May which made them ideal ammunition for the pea shooter. We would pull off a bunch and separate the buds from the stalks, place the buds in our mouths, then the tube of Cow Parsley stalk and blow hard. The spherical buds would then blast out of the pea shooter and travel some distance. Small boys could have great fun with these.

One year I found some stems which were bigger and longer than I normally found, and so I cut one of these to use as a pea shooter. I did not pay much attention to the purple spots on the stem and presumably did not notice the nasty smell and doubtless nasty taste. I was happy to have a bigger and better pea shooter than all the other boys. That night my lips swelled up, my throat was swollen and I was violently ill. I developed stomach cramps and then discovered a constant need for the smallest room in the house. I had made my pea shooter from Hemlock which is definitely not to be recommended. I have since found quite a few references to others who have mistaken Hemlock for Cow Parsley so it seems that I was not the only small boy to have suffered as a result!

Cow Parsley is also said to have associations with death and superstition holds that it should not be brought into the house as it will cause the death of a mother. This connection comes from the fact that Cow Parsley often grows on the site of graves in a churchyard.

SHINING CRANESBILL

Geranium lucidum

Shining Cranesbill

Shining Cranesbill is also sometimes called Shining Herb Robert. It is in the geranium family and as such has leaves and flowers typical of that genus, although the Shining Cranesbill flowers are smaller. It is a low-growing, annual plant, and often favours woodland where there are rocks or old walls. In these situations it can spread and climb if the rocks or walls have a suitably uneven surface. It favours alkaline areas, so is known as a calcicole.

The leaves do, in fact, shine, justifying its name. They often have a red tinge and the petioles and stalks are a deep red, so even when the plant is not in flower, it is attractive. The leaves are deeply indented and have an overall round shape. The indentations sub-divide the leaf into five main lobes and each lobe also has smaller indentations. This species is far less hairy than other species in the group and what hairs it does have are sparse and short. Presumably the shine is due to a thick cuticle and this is its way of preventing too much water loss from transpiration.

The flowers are pink with five petals and a calyx in the form of a capsule also made up of five fused sepals. Unlike many geranium species, the petals of Shining Cranesbill do not show an indentation at the top. Quite often the flower stalk is bent like a 'U' bend. It starts to flower in April.

Shining Cranesbill showing fused sepals

WILD STRAWBERRY
Fragaria vesca

The Wild Strawberry is in flower throughout the late spring and summer. It has a flower similar to the cultivated strawberry and goes on to produce little strawberries which are edible. There is a similar species which actually flowers earlier in the year called a Barren Strawberry, barren because it does not produce a fleshy red fruit. There is a difference between the flowers of these two in that the petals of the Wild Strawberry have very narrow gaps between them, whereas the petals of the Barren Strawberry are more clearly separated. The entry on the Barren Strawberry provides a comparison.

Once the season progresses then careful examination of the Wild Strawberry will reveal little developing fruits, probably green rather than red but still looking like little strawberries.

The Wild Strawberry is a perennial plant favouring dry, sometimes stony soil in woodland scrub. It will also grow in hedge banks, railway banks, roadsides and on basic rocky outcrops and screes in upland areas. It colonises open ground in quarries and chalk pits and grows on walls. It reproduces by seed as well as spreading by rooting runners or stolons. It is a common plant, partly due to the wide variety of habitats in which it can thrive.

The fruit is sometimes collected and eaten, although I find them fairly tasteless and too full of little pips. Compared to a cultivated strawberry, the wild variety is largely pip and very little fruit. The pips are actually little nuts or nutlets borne on the outside of the swollen receptacle.

Wild Strawberry

Wild Strawberry with developing fruits

WOODRUFF

Galium odoratum

Woodruff

Woodruff is in the group of plants which includes Bedstraws, Cleavers and Madder. Their leaves are arranged in whorls at intervals along the stem so there is a ring of 4-12 leaves, then a gap, then another ring and so on up the stem. This group are often climbing plants. They have fairly weak stems and rely on other plants or objects for support. The plants often have a rough texture due to the little hooks which help their scrambling activity.

Woodruff has a rough feel but it does not grow as high as Cleavers. It normally grows in a dense clump in which each stem helps support its neighbours and they grow up together. It has leaves arranged in whorls of about six. The flowers are white and small, as are most of the flowers in this group. Lady's Bedstraw is one exception, as it has yellow flowers; and Squinancywort has flowers which are vaguely pink. The Woodruff flowers are in bloom from April through to June and are of a sufficient size to make them quite easy to spot.

As might be anticipated, given its scientific name *odoratum*, this plant does have a smell which is sweet, rather like new-mown hay, and the smell increases as the plant dries. As a consequence it has various uses, the main one being inclusion in pot pourri. The scent helps to deter moths.

The active ingredient is coumarin, which is found in sweet vernal grass, meadowsweet and other plants. More exotic uses are as an ingredient in ice cream and in a German beer called Berliner Weisse.

Woodruff is a perennial plant so it grows in patches which gradually increase in size as the underground stolons spread outwards. It is also propagated by seeds which, as with others in this family, have little hooks on them which catch on clothes or on animal fur and get dispersed in that way.

WELSH POPPY

Meconopsis cambrica

Welsh Poppy

The Welsh poppy is a native species but the true native population is probably only found in Snowdonia and parts of Ireland. The BSBI suggests that it is only found in 54 of all the hectads that comprise Britain and those are all in Snowdonia. In Ireland it is found in 77 hectads. However the plant has established itself in the wild across Britain from garden-grown species, especially in northern regions.

Flowers shown in the photograph were growing in Wales but they were at the side of a track and close to some well-stocked gardens. They do however show the bright yellow which is typical of the wild type, whereas cultivated strains are often more orange yellow, some almost red. They favour damp shady places and are perennial plants.

The scientific names are interesting. Originally the Welsh Poppy was named *Papaver cambricum* by Linnaeus. Papaver is the genus that most of the other British species of poppies are in. Linnaeus was the scientist who invented the binomial system of naming all species.

Later, the flower was renamed *Meconopsis* because the structure of the stigma is slightly different to other poppies. Other poppies with a similarly shaped stigma were later found in Asia and the Himalayas. The popular blue poppy which is quite difficult to grow and often simply known as *Meconopsis* is one of them. Recent DNA analysis has shown that the Welsh poppy is not in fact related to the other Asian species but is actually related to the members of the Papaver genus. So Linnaeus got it right at the outset. So far some authorities have changed the name back to Papaver and others are still thinking about it.

The Welsh Poppy is the symbol for the Welsh Nationalist Party Plaid Cymru, who adopted it as their logo in 2006, replacing the previous logo which featured the Welsh dragon.

It is also the county wild flower for Merioneth in North Wales which is not surprising as a large part of the Snowdonia National Park lies within Merioneth, the one place where truly native Welsh Poppies seem to grow.

Welsh Poppy with developing seed pods

WATER AVENS
Geum rivale

Water Avens is a *Geum*. This group of plants is very popular with horticulturists and there are lots of different cultivars. Some are derived from *Geum rivale* but others have been bred from a related species called *Geum chiloense*.

The photograph shows the wild type and illustrates the nodding nature of these flowers. The petals are apricot. There is another species called Wood Avens or Herb Bennet which has smaller flowers with yellow petals and these two sometimes interbreed. In Honeypot Wood, a Norfolk Wildlife Trust reserve, both species grow separately, and as hybrids, some of which are quite beautiful and delicate.

Both species produce a seed head which has attractive hooked seeds. Hooked seeds are a common feature of woodland wild flowers, a practical trait since there are furry woodland animals that can effect seed dispersal. Seeds dispersed by wind are not so common in woodland wild flowers because woods are less windy than more exposed places. Those trees and shrubs in woodlands that do use wind as the method of dispersal have a height advantage.

Water Avens favour shady places and wet damp soils. I used to see it quite often when I lived in East Anglia but cannot recall ever having seen it growing wild in Gloucestershire, so I assume that it is less common here. I was very pleased therefore to discover it growing by a pond on a recent visit to South Lodge in Clearwell, Gloucestershire, part of the National Garden Scheme and a venue which opens regularly to the public and raises money for various worthwhile charities.

I generally think that most cultivars are not an improvement on the original wild type. They are usually bigger and brighter and in different colours but I think that they often lack the subtlety and delicacy of the wild species. It is, after all, the product of thousands of years of evolution, whereas the cultivar will be the product of just a few years of intensive cross pollination followed by a rapid breeding programme, a short advertising campaign, possibly an RHS medal, a few years of sales and often ultimate obscurity. Some *Geum* cultivars are, admittedly, quite attractive and may be worth the effort. I saw several examples of such varieties in the garden in Clearwell alongside the native species.

Water Avens seed head

Water Avens, the wild species

CLIMBING CORYDALIS

Ceratocapnos claviculata

This little plant is a common woodland species. It is not spectacular and I have not often seen it climbing, although it has fine delicate tendrils at the ends of its leaves which are presumably used for climbing. I like it for its delicate, almost tentative habit.

It is related to the Fumitories. Climbing Corydalis is the only native species of Corydalis in Britain.

Its flowers are small and white with a hint of yellow or brown. From a distance they look similar in shape to the flowers of Milkwort, and they also look like the Fumitory flowers as one would expect. The leaves are complex. Each little oval leaf is really a leaflet and is part of a larger compound leaf terminating in a little tendril.

I have seen it growing at most times of the year, certainly throughout the winter, and so it does not follow the normal pattern of an annual plant which would germinate in spring, grow and flower in summer, produce seeds in the autumn and then die. The photographs were taken in January and as can be seen the plant does have a few flowers.

Climbing Corydalis on a wall in Ninewells Wood

Climbing Corydalis

Most woodland plants are perennials as there is insufficient light available in one year to enable them to complete a life cycle and produce sufficient seed to ensure their survival through to the next year. As this is a plant which will survive for several seasons, it is not an annual in the strict sense of the word. In my wood, before it was cleared of Pines, it was one of the field layer plants which seemed to cope well under a dense woodland canopy.

There is a small weevil which lives on it called the Climbing Corydalis Weevil, *Procas granulicollis*. This Weevil is rare, with only a few recorded sightings throughout Britain. Highest numbers occur from late April to the end of June, but more research is needed on this weevil.

WOOD STITCHWORT

Stellaria nemorum

Wood Stitchwort

Stitchworts and Chickweeds are both in the Caryophyllaceae family, commonly known as the Campion, Pink or Carnation family. *Stellaria* is the genus of Stitchworts and Chickweeds and Wood Stitchwort is very similar to another species in the same genus called Greater Chickweed. With Wood Stitchwort the key feature is the sepals are much shorter than the petals. Wood Stitchwort is also sometimes known as Wood Chickweed.

This perennial plant comes into flower in early May, a little later than its larger relative Greater Stitchwort which begins to flower in mid-April. The flowers are similar in that both are pure white and have five petals which are deeply notched but the petals of Wood Stitchwort are thinner and more floppy than the more robust petals of Greater Stitchwort.

Wood Stitchwort has ten stamens and three stigmas. Other diagnostic features of this perennial plant are that the lower leaves have well-developed leaf stalks (petioles); the main stalks are hairy and have hairs all over the stem, not arranged in two rows as is the case with Greater Chickweed. Finally the Wood Stitchwort flower stalks are not as long as those of Greater Chickweed.

Wood Stitchwort is quite rare, mainly found in the north of England and southern Scotland. It is only present in just over 400 of the 2810 hectads that make up Britain and Ireland and is virtually absent in the south of Britain.

LEOPARDSBANE

Doronicum sp.

There are quite a lot of species of Doronicum or Leopardsbane. None of them are native to Britain and most come from Central and Eastern Asia. As with many garden plants, they have escaped into the wild and established themselves. They are all yellow daisy-like plants, some flower early in the year which makes them popular with gardeners. In addition they are easy to grow and will tolerate shady places.

Their distribution is not uniform and they are most likely to be found in the eastern regions of Scotland and along the Welsh/English border. They are easy to spot when flowering in May to July, with their bold yellow flowers. In the wild they grow 30–45cm high and are normally found in hedgerows or woodland edges.

The three most common species found in Britain are *Doronicum pardalianches*, which is the type encountered most often, then there is *D. plantagineum* Plantain-leaved Leopardsbane which has longer thinner leaves, and finally *D. columnae* Eastern Leopardsbane which has heart-shaped leaves.

As for its common name, 'bane' means banish. Fleabane was incorporated into straw bedding years ago as it was thought to deter fleas. There is also a plant called Dogsbane and yes that is thought to deter dogs. Wolfsbane is in the Aconitum family and is deadly poisonous. Extracts of it were used to add to bait in the past to get rid of wolves and other predatory animals which might cause problems to sheep flocks.

There is a suggestion that Leopardsbane, which is poisonous, should not be planted in a garden in which a tortoise is kept: if it eats the leaves, that could kill it.

Leopardsbane

Leopardsbane by the River Severn

COMMON BISTORT

Persicaria bistorta

Common Bistort, wild stock

This Bistort was growing in a dark area of a small wooded nature reserve. The plant is common, especially in the west of the country, augmented by many garden escapees, so maybe the rather spindly specimens growing in the nature reserve are true wild stock and the bigger, bolder plants one often sees are related to garden varieties.

This plant has a host of other common names such as Gentle Dock, Passion Dock, Pudding Dock and Patience Dock. The leaves look very similar to those of Dock. The name Bistort derives from *bis* as in twice and *torta* for twisted as the root is supposed to twist round twice. This is also the derivation of its other common name of Snakeroot.

Common Bistort, garden variety

HERB PARIS

Paris quadrifolia

Herb Paris, a fine flowering specimen

Herb Paris is an odd-looking plant. It is only found in ancient woodlands. It generally has just four leaves which are aligned opposite one another in two pairs which is the reason for the name Paris. It has nothing to do with the capital of France. The distinctive leaf pattern makes Herb Paris fairly easy to spot, although occasionally it has three or even five leaves.

It typically grows in the company of Dog's Mercury, Wood Anemone, Violets and Bluebells. It grows in small patches and is often obscured by large swathes of Dog's Mercury. Along with several other woodland plants it seems to benefit from living in Coppice-with-Standards woodland. The effect of the coppicing cycle is to cause a burst of growth in the plants in the few years immediately after coppicing and then a decline as the coppiced bushes grow back up and the shade increases. On the plus side, the shade also eliminates competitive species such as brambles and nettles.

A peculiarity of this plant is its flower. It has eight stamens, four stigmas and four seed capsules which are symmetrically arranged. This balance and symmetry led to it being used to exemplify marriage as a balanced and equal relationship.

The four larger green appendages are sepals. The petals are narrow (filiform) and again there are four. There are eight stamens with brown stalks and yellow colour from the pollen, and finally there are four dark brown stigmas. It flowers in May and June and is normally found in alkaline and damp conditions.

The plant produces just one dark purple fruit in the centre which resembles a blueberry but it is poisonous and tastes unpleasant, so there is little risk of people eating it.

RED CAMPION

Silene dioica

After the main show of Bluebells and Ramsons are over, the woods and hedgerows settle down for a while and during late spring and summer no single plant fully dominates. On the fringe of woodlands, the Cow Parsley and the Red Campion are the most obvious wild flowers. Red Campion continues to flower right through the summer and well into the autumn.

Red Campion is predominantly a flower of the hedgerows and is not found in the deep shade of a woodland. However, a woodland glade which is, after all, environmentally much the same as a hedgerow, is a place where they are often found.

They can grow to just over a metre if in a favourable position. The leaves and stem are hairy, giving the foliage a greyish-green appearance. The flowers are not red but pink

Red Campion

It is potentially useful because the roots can be boiled to make a good substitute for soap due to the saponin content. It has been particularly used to wash delicate fabrics like fine linen and silk. It was traditionally considered to be a cure for snakebites.

Red Campion has an association with St James as it often in full bloom on 25 July, which is his feast day.

Growing beside a gate at Ninewells Wood

and the male and female flowers are borne on different plants.

There is also a White Campion, *Silene latifolia,* but it is not shade tolerant. It sometimes hybridises with Red Campion.

Red Campion flowers produce a capsule full of seeds and dispersal is by the pepper pot mechanism whereby the heavy seed pod held up on a thin stalk is shaken about in the wind and the seeds are flung out a metre or so, as in the case of poppies. From there, clumps or patches of plants develop. The plant is a biennial, flowering in its second year but it will linger on for several years. A similar plant is Ragged Robin *Silene flos-cuculi* which grows mainly in damp, dappled woodland.

Red Campion is a common wild flower and has a host of alternative names, including Bachelor's Buttons, Billy Buttons, Adder's Flower, Drunkards, Gramfer-greygles, Red Riding Hood, Robin Hood and Scalded Apples.

It is an ancient woodland indicator (*see page 246*).

Cleavers

CLEAVERS

Galium aparine

Cleavers is a very common woodland edge and hedgerow plant as well as being a tiresome weed. It will grow in woodlands as long as the conditions are not too shady.

Perhaps not surprisingly given that it is such a common plant, it has a lot of names: Goosegrass, Sticky Willy, Clivers, Bedstraw, Catchweed, Gripgrass, Robin Run the Hedge, Sticky Willow, Bort, Stickyweed, Stickybud, Stickyjack and Sticklejack – so quite a few!

Scientifically it is in the Bedstraw family and as such it has square stems with its leaves arranged in whorls, normally 6-8 lance-shaped leaves per whorl. The flowers are very small and white and composed of four pointed petals. They start to flower in May and continue in bloom throughout the summer. The flowers are often produced singly or in twos or threes on short side shoots, but can also be produced terminally.

The plant has little backward-pointing hairs on the stems and leaves which give it a rough feel and cause it to stick to clothing or the fur of animals. The seeds are also covered with little sticky hairs. The little burrs are often referred to as sweethearts. When I was a child we had a long-haired tabby cat called 'Tailsy'. I have no idea where that name came from. Tailsy used to get lots of sweethearts in his fur and it was really difficult to get them out. Sometimes a whole chunk of fur had to be cut out with a pair of scissors. This shows how efficiently this helps to disperse the seeds, the more so if they get caught on the fur of an animal such as a dog or deer with short hair or on the clothes of humans.

Cleaver seeds contain caffeine and if one collects a sufficient amount, then gently roasts and grinds them, they are said to make a passable cup of coffee. I've never tried it: it's a lot of time and effort to gather a sufficient quantity of seeds to make just one cup of coffee!

Cleavers showing a flower, backwards hairs, black flies and an ant.

RAGGED ROBIN

Silene flos-cuculi

Ragged Robin is an iconic little wild flower, and I am delighted that there is one plant of it growing in my area of woodland.

I first saw it some years ago and it has continued to grow in the same place each year which is not surprising as it is classified as a perennial. Ragged Robin grows in a variety of habitats which include damp areas of lightly shaded woodland. I have seen it growing in such conditions in Norfolk and in my own wood in Monmouthshire and in other nearby woods.

I remember taking various groups of students to a damp wet woodland on the edge of Shouldham Warren which was part of the estate of Sir Thomas Hare. It is near Downham Market in Norfolk and my visits took place in the 1980s. It was an area consisting of Alder Carr and Silver Birch, with some young Oak, full of fantastic mosses and absolutely beautiful. There were just a few woodland flowering species there which included Marsh Valerian, Hemp Agrimony... and Ragged Robin.

Ragged Robin

Each school group which visited my centre would be accompanied by a couple of their teachers. One of these teachers was a nice chap, a very good teacher, but someone not to be argued with; he decided that some of the Ragged Robins would be better served if he dug them up and transplanted them into his garden in Worksop. I said nothing at the time, and maybe as a way to haunt me, the single Ragged Robin has decided to grow in my patch of Ninewells Wood, a reminder of my reluctance to speak out on behalf of the Ragged Robin all those years ago.

The flowers appear from May to August and are a good source of nectar for butterflies and bumble bees. Subsequent to pollination, a small rounded capsule is produced which contains lots of seeds. These are dispersed using the pepper pot mechanism.

Despite the one plant in my woodland flowering now for several years, no new plants have appeared. Maybe I should lend a helping hand and collect a small number of seeds to plant them in a pot of soil at home and, if any grow. I can plant them back out in the woods. Then perhaps I will have made up for the ones that were dug up in Norfolk all those years ago and my conscience can at last be cleared.

Ragged Robin's official status is 'declining' due to agricultural practices and I for one wish this joyous plant of damp places a strong and speedy recovery.

This species used to be called *Lychnis flos-cuculi* until 2015 when it was officially changed to *Silene flos-cuculi*.

LILY OF THE VALLEY
Convallaria majalis

Lily of the Valley is a native species and, because it is so beautiful and smells so delightful, it has been grown in gardens for generations. The garden specimens have steadily infiltrated the countryside. The true wild types tend to be a bit more leggy than garden varieties. However, no doubt soil conditions, and available light also affect their stature.

The Lily of the Valley's preferred habitat is partial shade, light well-drained soil which is slightly alkaline and with plenty of humus. However, finding an alkaline soil with humus is quite a tall order, and so it is a rare and beautiful sight in a woodland if you do come across a clump of Lily of the Valley growing there.

The scent is an ingredient in Dior perfume, and is popular in wedding bouquets including recent royal weddings.

Lily of the Valley

ROUGH CHERVIL

Chaerophyllum temulum

Rough Chervil is one of several Umbellifers which all look rather similar. This one is easily mistaken for Cow Parsley. But it is more delicate than Cow Parsley and the rough stems are a more reddish purple. This purple colouration can appear in the form of blotches, and then it looks a bit like Hemlock. Rough Chervil is poisonous although not quite as deadly as Hemlock. The sap can cause blistering on the skin and if eaten, the symptoms are similar to drunkenness. Cattle and other grazers sometimes eat it and suffer as a result. Another related species is Chervil, the garden herb with a delicate flavour: a hint of liquorice which is part of the French *fines herbes* mix and is a substitute for parsley. It is clearly important that one does not confuse Chervil with Rough Chervil.

Rough Chervil flowers from May to July, by which time it can be about 100cm high, so not the tallest of the group. Generally, a little later to flower than Cow Parsley, it is a biennial species, so is reliant on producing a good number of seeds each year to maintain its population. As a result, it is not suited to the dark conditions in the heart of woodland but restricted to the woodland margins. It is not so keen on very wet or acidic soils.

The flowers are attractive to various insects, especially hoverflies, which pick up pollen by crawling across the surface of the umbel thereby transferring the pollen from flower to flower and plant to plant.

Rough Chervil

GROUND ELDER

Aegopodium podagraria

Ground Elder is one of the white woodland fringe and hedgerow umbellifers that help to give that early summer look to our lanes and byways. It is so called because the leaves look like those of the bush Elder, but they do not have Elder's disgusting smell.

At a casual glance it might be mistaken for Cow Parsley, but the leaves are completely different and there are subtle differences in the flowers. They tend to be at their best in the first week of June, by which time the Cow Parsley is going over. Ground Elder is slightly shorter and 'neater' than Cow Parsley. The individual umbels are more contained, they are smaller and there are fewer of them. They appear brighter white than Cow Parsley, perhaps because the individual flowers that make up the umbel are more closely packed.

Ground Elder in flower

Ground Elder prior to flowering

Ground Elder is invasive and difficult to eradicate. I remember we had it growing in our garden when I was a boy and my father used to spend a lot of time trying to dig it up. It spreads with underground rhizomes which matt together making it difficult to dig into and preventing anything else from growing. If one digs up the rhizomes, then every little piece accidentally left in the ground produces a new plant and soon one is back to where one started. I do not think my father ever got the better of it. However it grew in a fairly dark area of the garden where probably not much else would have grown so I wonder why he bothered.

Ground Elder does have its uses. The plant is said to have been introduced into Britain by the Romans as a food plant and as a medicinal herb by monks. Apparently it can be used in the same way as spinach if the leaves are collected when they are tender and first appear, in February through to late May. Once the leaves are older they have a bad taste and can act as a laxative.

BLACK BRYONY

Tamus communis

Black Bryony's scientific name is *Tamus communis*, sometimes referred to as *Dioscorea communis*. Bryon is a Celtic name, meaning brave or virtuous.

It climbs up through other plants, wrapping its stem around them. Black Bryony has heart-shaped, shiny leaves. The fruits of the Black Bryony are poisonous, shiny and bright red when ripe. It is in the same family as yams and has an underground tuber.

The flowers of the Black Bryony are small and arranged in a string. The plants are either all male or all female (dioecious).

It is well distributed in woodlands throughout England although it becomes more rare north of Manchester and it is very rarely found in Scotland.

Black Bryony in flower

Black Bryony with fruits

WHITE BRYONY

Bryonia dioica

This is the other one of two Bryony species that may be encountered in woods and hedgerows, the other being Black Bryony. The two plants are not related.

The flowers are a greenish white with the veins showing up in green. They have five petals and the male and female flowers are borne on separate plants, hence its name *dioica*. The petals are covered with short hairs which is somewhat unusual. This species is in fact in the cucumber and marrow family *Cucurbitaceae* and is the only wild species of this family found in Britain.

The ripe red berries are quickly eaten by birds which is why one does not often see them. The berries have little white hairs on them. Despite all parts of the plant being poisonous to humans, the leaves are often full of holes as they are eaten by a variety of insects.

White Bryony flower

White Bryony with spiral tendrils

PIGNUT

Conopodium majus

Pignut is an umbellifer. It is a small plant which can tolerate fairly dark conditions, so it is a regular woodland species. It would be unlikley to grow in hedgerows as taller grasses and plants such as Cow Parsley, Stinging Nettles and Red Campion would swamp it.

As the name suggests, it is edible and the 'nut' is in fact an underground tuber. In general I do not approve of digging up and disturbing wild flowers. Foraging Pignuts will destroy it whereas taking a few leaves from something like Wild Garlic to add to a stew or blend into a soup will not do it any

Pignut

permanent damage. I always remember my mother telling me that they used to gather baskets full of Cowslip flowers to make wine when she was younger. Then she would add that 'now of course you hardly ever see any'! Whether it was the collection that resulted in their scarcity or changes in farming practice or herbicides I do not know, probably a combination of the two, but certainly gathering them by the basketful would not have helped.

The 'nut' is buried deep below the surface. No doubt this is beneficial to the plant as it makes extracting it quite difficult, thus protecting it from smaller foragers like squirrels, mice and hedgehogs. Obviously larger mammals such as pigs, badgers and, where I live, wild boar, will easily be able to dig down the 15–20cm required to gain access.

Despite there being lots of wild boar living in the Forest of Dean, there are also lots of Pignuts there, so they have not had too detrimental an effect on their population – yet! There were two releases of wild boar, one in the 1990s near Ross on Wye and a second in 2004 near the village of Staunton and now they are established and found everywhere in the region.

The Pignut has small, highly divided and slightly darker green leaves. The flowers are out in May and June with little white umbels, but unlike many species in this group, the outer florets in the umbel do not have larger petals than the florets in the centre. They all seem to be roughly the same size. The leaves are very fine and dark green, more like asparagus rather than like the 'ferny' leaves of Cow Parsley.

Showing its thin, divided foliage

FRINGE CUPS

Tellima grandiflora

Fringe Cup flower head

The flowers of Fringe Cups, a member of the Saxifrage family, are arranged on a spike, similar to those of Agrimony. When you look closely at the individual flowers, they have five petals and each is highly fringed: quite unusual.

Often the flowers develop a pink or reddish colour, and it is normally the flowers at the bottom of the spike which exhibit that most.

The flower spikes often curl over at the top.

Fringe Cups showing pink petal edges

COLUMBINE
Aquilegia vulgaris

Columbine

Columbine is a native British plant. I once saw a patch of it growing along a woodland roadside. When the vegetation was being cut, the tractor driver had obviously been so impressed by this small group of about four plants that he had cut round them and left them in all their glory. They stood about 1.5m tall and were covered with large dark purple and blue flowers. I have only seen the wild purple version growing a few times. There are lots of Columbine growing in Britain but most of them are not the true wild variety. Most are various shades of pink; some even have semi double flowers. They all seem to have been affected by the various garden varieties.

The BSBI seems to have given up on differentiating between true native Columbine plants and 'garden' types. They say '*A. vulgaris has increased since the 1962 Atlas, presumably because of the increasing frequency of garden escapes. The native distribution is now totally obscured and all records are mapped as if they were native.*'

My father used to have Aquilegias in the garden, which grew to about half a metre high. The flowers will have been bred by gardeners from the original wild stock, but I contend that no Aquilegia is an improvement on the original.

Another name for Columbine is Old Ladies Bonnet, due to the shape of the flower. It prefers the less shady areas of woodlands, and so is often seen along woodland rides or in hedgerows.

BASTARD BALM

Melittis melissophyllum

Bastard Balm

What a shame it has this name! It has to be one of the most attractive of the Nettle family and in my opinion it rivals many of the British Orchids for beauty. Indeed, superficially it looks like an Orchid.

The plant has the name because the leaves bear a close resemblance to the leaves of Lemon Balm *Melissa officinalis* which was originally known just as Balm and this has been grown in gardens for about 500 years. It is also sometimes known as Common Balm or Balm Mint. Lemon Balm is a very useful herb, much used in cooking. Adding a sprig of it to stewed rhubarb improves the flavour.

Bastard Balm, on the other hand, has hardly any smell. It is in the large group of plants commonly known as the Labiates, meaning that the flower has a lip. It is similar to White Dead Nettle except that the flowers of Bastard Balm are much bigger and have a pink lip. The plant is scarce in Britain as we are at the northern limit of its range, but it is relatively common in Devon. It is also available to buy as a garden perennial and various cultivars exist, including an all-white cultivar.

It is a good woodland plant as it is very attractive to bees. The large lip serves as their landing pad and the pink colour helps to direct them in. It has been used over the ages and in various countries as a cure for a vast range of ailments. There is some scientific evidence that it contains a number of active ingredients which may well be beneficial. One study found that the essential oil from the leaves could be used for its sedative, narcotic, antifungal and antibacterial effects and that it is a muscle relaxant and spasmolytic.

The scientific name derives from *melitta* which is Greek for bee and is a reference to this species being particularly favoured by honey bees. Bastard Balm is the only member of the genus *Melittis* and it is quite unusual for a genus to only have one species in it.

Bastard Balm growing among Purple Gromwell (blue flowers)

Stinging Nettles

STINGING NETTLE
Urtica dioica

'Urtica because they 'urt you.' I remember Professor David Bellamy saying this once on a television programme. A good way to remember the Latin name, but in fact 'Urtica' comes from the Latin verb *urere*, meaning 'to burn'.

There are two species of Urtica in Britain, the Common or Stinging Nettle and the Small Nettle. Both sting and look quite similar, but the Small Nettle is an annual and grows in more open places. The Common Nettle is a perennial and grows in a range of places, often found in hedgerows and open woodlands. Perhaps the most relevant condition for its growth is a high level of nitrogen and potassium in the soil, so it is often found where man has been active in the past or where there has been a bonfire. Rosebay Willowherb and Sheep's Sorrel are also often associated with woodland bonfire sites.

The species name '*dioica*' indicates that there are separate male and female plants and the flowers of each are different. They are not attractive to insects but use wind pollination. As such, the flowers are long and dangly, rather like those of Oak trees, an example of parallel evolution.

I used to take my students to an area of Norfolk called Foulden Common, which is a Site of Special Scientific Interest. It has chalk grassland, fens, carr woodland and deciduous woodland. It also has a little stream and some special features called pingoes. In the early years of my visits there I sometimes met an old local gentleman walking a black and white dog. He used to tell me the history and ecology of the common. He had been a Fen Reeve which is like a Sheriff, an elected member of the community with responsibility for the management of the Common including the fen area. He said that in days gone by, they used to lay the hedges and this work involved the men getting stung regularly by nettles. These men never developed rheumatism in their old age. He also told me, with something of a twinkle in his eye, that local people would strip naked and

In flower

beat themselves with nettles. This was done at certain times of year as a ritual. It caused the skin to glow and a warm sensation would ensue. I have not tried it, but further research reveals that urtication, or flogging with nettles, is the process of deliberately applying stinging nettles to the skin in order to provoke inflammation. An agent thus used is known as a rubefacient (which causes redness) and is a folk remedy for the treatment of rheumatism.

Nettles produce a powerful network of underground rhizomes which spread rapidly and effectively. They also have very strong and spreading roots which are a characteristic bright yellow.

Nettle soup is well known, and I have tried making it a few times: one needs to use young nettle shoots. The only place that I have sampled a delicious version of this soup was in the Dordogne, but the majority of nettle soups are sadly are not so tasty.

Nettles are the food plant for various butterfly caterpillars including Peacock, Small Tortoiseshell, Red Admiral and Comma, and it is an often-quoted notion that leaving a wild patch in the garden is good for the butterflies. Rubbish! The controlling factor on the population of butterflies whose caterpillars feed on nettles is not food source. There is hardly a shortage of nettles for consumption. Given the population of nettles in woodlands and countryside, we should be overrun with Peacock and Tortoiseshell butterflies. Leaving a patch of nettles at the end of the garden is not going to make any difference. A variety of other factors including winter temperatures, pesticides, places to hibernate and predators probably controls their numbers, but availability of nettles is not going to be anywhere in the top ten.

SANICLE
Sanicula europaea

Sanicle showing buttercup-like leaves

I t may sound like a lavatory cleaning product, but Sanicle is in fact a small and delicate member of the Umbellifer group. It starts to flower in May and June and continues to bloom until August. It has neat, almost spherical umbels rather than the typical wide umbrella shape. The stamens, which are initially folded in on themselves, eventually open up giving the flower head a star-like appearance. It is a member of the carrot family and grows in moist deciduous woodland, particularly Oak, Beech and Ash.

This woodland plant usually has white flowers, but I have also seen some with a pinkish hue.

The leaves are more like buttercup leaves; chunky, hairless and shiny, features technically known as glaborous.

The seeds, as with many woodland plants, are dispersed by hooks which catch on the fur of animals. The name 'sanicle' is derived from the Latin '*sanus*' meaning 'healthy', relating to its value as a medicinal plant. Tutsan is a plant with a name that has a similar derivation, *tout sain* in French literally meaning all-healthy.

Sanicle showing stamens opening

COMMON FIGWORT

Scrophularia nodosa

Common Figwort comes into flower in June. It has small flowers that are well spaced apart in the form of a spike. The individual flowers are purple, almost brown, and resemble a truncated Foxglove or Deadly Nightshade. If in doubt, check the stem. Figwort has a square stem, whilst the stem of Deadly Nightshade is circular.

This species prefers to grow where it is wet or at least damp. It can tolerate heavy shade and therefore can be found deep in the woods.

The Common Figwort is favoured by various insects attracted to a rather unpleasant smell produced by the flowers. There is a little weevil which feeds on it, aptly named the Figwort weevil *Cionus scrophulariae*. A caterpillar which is the larva of the Mullein Moth *Cucullia verbasci* also uses it as a food source, so if one comes across this plant then it is worth giving it a close look to see what else might be there.

There are several other species of Figwort which are found in woodland, including Water Figwort *Scrophularia auriculata*, Green Figwort *Scrophularia umbrosa* and Balm-leaved Figwort *Scrophularia scorodonia.* They are all rare and the flowers are all fairly similar. But Water Figwort is trifoliate, Green Figwort has simple leaves but they are more indented than the Common Figwort and its square stem has fringed edges. Finally Balm-leaved Figwort has leaves that are hairy.

Common Figwort

Spike of Common Figwort

BITTERCRESS
Cardamine species

There are four species of Bittercress. They are all shade-tolerant and not only found in woodlands but also in gardens where they are regarded as weeds. In order of abundance there is Hairy Bittercress *C. hirsuta*, Wavy Bittercress *C. flexuosa*, Large Bittercress *C. amara* and, the least common, Narrow-leaved Bittercress *C. impatiens*.

Hairy Bittercress
This is most prolific of the bittercresses, both in woodlands and as a garden weed. If not weeded out early, the seed pod bursts, and a shower of little seeds are dispersed, thus creating another generation of bittercress in a month or so. Key features of this species that help to differentiate it are a straight stem and seed pods which develop to extend well beyond the flowers when blooming. The little flowers have four stamens but would probably require a hand lens to see them. It can grow to a height of 15cm and flowers throughout the year.

Wavy Bittercress
The stem grows in a zig-zag fashion which gives it its name. The seed pods tend not to grow up as high above the remaining flowers, as with Hairy Bittercress. The flowers have six stamens, and flowering is more restricted between April to September. It is even more likely to be found in woodland, favouring wet, muddy or boggy ground. Wavy Bittercress stems are hairy. It has a strong smell of watercress when the leaves are damaged. This plant can grow to a height of almost 30cm.

I recently came across **Large Bittercress** growing on the banks of the River Wey in Guildford alongside a wooded region which was shaded and boggy. Due to its height it was fairly easy to spot – it can grow up to 60cm. It bears some resemblance to Cuckooflower, to which it is related. The flowers are white, with purple stamens.

Narrow-leaved Bittercress
The least common of the four species, it is usually restricted to woodland. I have found it growing alongside shaded woodland paths, in parts of central England, but rarely in Wales or Ireland, and not at all in Scotland. It has very small petals which are sometimes absent altogether. The anthers are yellow which makes the tiny flowers look yellow. It is hairless and has deeply toothed leaves. This is also a woodland species.

Right: A mossy bank from which is growing Wavy and Narrow-leaved Bitttercress

Wavy Bittercress

Large Bittercress

Narrow-leaved Bittercress
flower head

SPEEDWELLS

Veronica species

Thyme-leaved Speedwell

Speedwells are very pretty little flowers which range in colour from bright blue through to purple and a few are almost white. There are over twenty different species and many of them live in disturbed or cultivated land but there are five which are particularly found in woodlands.

To explain some of the terminology: a petiole is the leaf stalk and a raceme describes flowers which are arranged up a central stem with each flower attached to the main stem by its own little stem. I list here the five Speedwells. There are far more similarities than differences which makes identification challenging so anything which is a specific characteristic for a particular woodland species, I have underlined and identified which type of woodland.

Ivy-leaved Speedwell

Ivy-leaved Speedwell

Veronica hederifolia
Flowers: solitary, 4-9mm across
Stems and Petiole: both hairy
Leaves: <u>ivy-shaped</u> with 1–3 large teeth
Habitat: open woods, hedgerows, woodland walls and banks

Ivy-leaved Speedwell

Thyme-leaved Speedwell: detail

Thyme-leaved Speedwell
Veronica serpyllifolia sub-species *serpyllifolia*
Flowers: in racemes, 5-10mm across, pale blue with darker veins
Stems and Petiole: up to 30cm high. <u>No petioles</u>
Leaves: oval to elliptical, <u>non-hairy</u>
Habitat: woodland rides

Germander or Bird's-eye Speedwell
Veronica chamaedrys
Flowers: in racemes, 8-12mm across, bright blue, with a white 'eye'
Stems and Petiole: up to 50cm high, petioles short (5mm) or absent and <u>stems with two opposite lines of hairs</u>
Leaves: triangular to oval, serrated and hairy
Habitat: woods, hedgerows

Germander Speedwell

Germander Speedwell

Heath Speedwell

Wood Speedwell
Veronica montana
Flowers: in racemes, 8-10mm across, lilac or blue
Stems and petioles: up to 40cm high, hairy all over, petioles 5-15mm
Leaves: oval to broadly oval, deeply serrated and hairy.
Habitat: damp woodlands

Nothing is totally definitive, it is just a case of looking at a combination of flower size and colour along with leaf shape, all of which can vary in any given species and often does.

Heath Speedwell

Heath Speedwell
Veronica officinalis
Flowers: in racemes, 5-9mm across, lilac
Stems and petioles: up to 40cm high, hairy all over, petioles present but only just!
Leaves: oval to elliptical, mildly serrated and hairy
Habitat: open woods, banks and heathland

Wood Speedwell

Wood Speedwell

UPRIGHT SPURGE

Euphorbia serrulata

Upright Spurge

Upright Spurge is quite a rarity and the only place it is found growing as a native plant as opposed to a garden escapee is in the Wye Valley around Tintern and in the Forest of Dean. Recently I was walking in some local Forestry Commission woods when I noticed some spurge plants growing in the centre of a forestry track, in the strip down the middle which does not get trampled so much and where little plants can survive. These little spurges looked a bit different to the ones I had seen before, so I took a few photographs. In the past I have seen lots of Woodland Spurge.

Later on my walk I came across several more plants growing at the edge of the woodland track and here they were a bit taller, maybe up to 40cm high. I took more photographs and on researching them I was pleased to discover that they were the Upright Spurge, also sometimes known as the Tintern Spurge because of where it is found.

To put its rarity into context, the BSBI says it is only recorded in 13 of the 2810 hectads that make up Great Britain and only one hectad in the whole of Ireland. That really is quite rare!

I saw 10-15 Upright Spurge that day, all in flower. The seed pods are covered with little green warty protuberances. These were only just visible as the seeds had yet to develop. The leaf shape is broadly oval with a blunt point which is characteristic of this species. In subsequent years I have found large numbers some years and in other years, just a few.

Showing warty protuberances on the seed heads

SOLOMON'S SEAL

Polygonatum multiflorum

Solomon's Seal, P. multiflorum

There are three species of Solomon's Seal growing in Britain but one of them, Whorled Solomon Seal, is very rare and only found in Scotland.

Of the other two, the Angular Solomon's Seal has square stems in cross-section, the bell-shaped flowers are not nipped in halfway down the tube part and the flowers are usually borne singly.

Solomon's Seal has round stems, the tube part of the flower has a marked restriction halfway down and there are usually three flowers at each position. The hybrid, *P. hybridum (below)* was growing in the wild. It has a slight narrowing of the tube, it has ridged but not square stems and two flowers at each position, so it is exactly mid-way between the two wild species. The hybrid is the one I come across most often, presumably as a garden escape.

The true Solomon's Seal is relatively rare and has only been recorded in 268 hectads in the whole of Britain.

Solomon's Seal gets a lot of plaudits from herbalists and alternative medicine practitioners, and is currently being researched as a possible source of remedies for heart conditions. In the past it was used to heal bruises and the flowers were distilled and used to remove spots from the skin.

There are several explanations for the name of Solomon's Seal and they all seem to relate to the peculiar marks or depressions found on the rhizomatous roots which are said to resemble the Seal of Solomon. It is probably best not to dig them up and check out the rhizomes though.

The hybrid variety growing wild, Polygonatum hybridium

SPIKED STAR OF BETHLEHEM

Ornithogalum pyrenaicum

This species is native but fairly scarce. It is sometimes known as Bath Asparagus which gives a clue as to where it grows in Britain.

Spiked Star of Bethlehem is normally found growing in shady woodland habitats and it is more common in France and Spain. In Britain it is only found in a few places, just 33 of the 2810 hectads. It is found around Bath and in a few locations east of there, and also in a small zone in Bedfordshire. In France it is very common, and can often be seen along country roads in shaded areas. If there is woodland on both sides of the road it is often present. It dislikes too much light.

Before they come into bloom, they resemble thin spikes of asparagus, hence its common name, Bath Asparagus. It was once gathered and sold in markets in Bath for consumption, and is still eaten in some countries on the Continent, although I understand that there are suspicions that it may be slightly poisonous. As this is a rare plant in Britain, collecting it here is not a good idea and probably illegal. Nevertheless, it was being sold in Bath until the early 1970s in a greengrocers owned by an elderly couple.

Its flower spikes usually bear twenty or more flowers.

Spiked Star of Bethlehem

EARLY SUMMER

(JUNE)

This is the season where the flowers of the woodland edges really make a show. We have already enjoyed the white and frothy Cow Parsley, Ground Elder and Rough Chervil following on one from the other and now we are into the season of Hogweed, which is normally white, but it sometimes shows a distinct pink colour. It is much loved by a vast array of insects, all feasting on the nectar and inadvertently carrying out the pollination. Possibly this is the most diverse period for woodland flower species as there will still be straggling late flowering plants from earlier months and these will be joined by the long-distance runners such as White Dead Nettle and Red Campion which will struggle on right through to October. There will be other wild flowers showing now that flower a bit later in the year but one or two of their number will inevitably set off before the starting pistol has been fired.

It is well worth a foray during the early summer into even the darkest, gloomiest regions of the woods as there are some gems to be found. Birds Nest Orchid and Yellow Birds Nest are two such species. They have similar names and are superficially similar, but they are not related. What they have in common is that they are both parasitic and rely on stealing food from trees. As such they have no chlorophyll, they are yellowy brown and are not dependant on light, so they can grow and flower in the darkest regions of the woods.

There are other species with a similar lifestyle such as Ivy Broomrape which is a woodland species. There are some very special woodland flowers appearing in early summer such as the Martagon Lily or the Greater Butterfly Orchid which can require some diligent searching, but if all else fails, just marvel at the prolific splendour of the Foxgloves.

Common Spotted Orchid

COMMON COW-WHEAT

Melampyrum pratense

Cow-wheat is an attractive little plant. It has yellow flowers which are on show for a long period over the summer, for a woodland plant, from May to September. Most woodland plants have finished flowering by June.

It will also grow in scrubland, heaths and moors.

Common Cow-wheat is an annual herb and a hemi-parasitic plant, meaning that it obtains some of its nutrients from the roots of nearby plants, in the same way as Bartsia and Yellow Rattle do. This is quite unusual for a woodland plant.

Most woodland wild flowers are perennials because the restricted amount of light available in one season in a woodland is not enough for the plant to efficiently germinate, grow, flower and produce sufficient seed all in one season. So well done, the Cow-wheat! It has obviously managed to accomplish all this and to achieve it each and every year, otherwise it would have become extinct long ago.

It is usually found on the edge of a woodland where there is a bit more light.

Common Cow-wheat

There are several Cow-wheat species growing in Britain but only Common Cow-wheat is associated with woodlands. It is found throughout most of Britain whereas the other species such as Small Cow-wheat, Crested Cow-wheat and Field Cow-wheat are quite rare and have a very restricted range.

Common Cow-wheat is a real indicator of ancient woodland. In Oliver Rackham's list of species which occur most often in ancient woodland, this species comes sixth, and was recorded in fourteen out of the eighteen areas that he investigated.

The reason for this plant being restricted to ancient woodland is that its seed dispersal is dependant on wood ants and ants will not carry seed very far, certainly not the hundreds of yards necessary to enable it to pass from one woodland to another. As a result it is very difficult for the plant to spread further, so the Cow-wheat remains where it has been for the last hundreds of years, that is to say in its ancient woodland home, and it will be almost impossible for it to colonise a newly planted woodland.

The seeds resemble wheat seeds, hence the name, but they also look a bit like the ants' pupae which is part of the reason why ants pick them up. The seed has an elaiosome, which is a special little part that the ants like to eat. The ants collect up the seeds and take them back to their nests. The elaiosome, which is rich in lipids and proteins, is fed to their larvae.

Cow-wheat is also the food plant of the caterpillars of the Heath Fritillary butterfly.

Common Cow-wheat flower head

HOGWEED

Heracleum sphondylium

Hogweed, despite its unflattering name, is attractive close up. Usually it has white flowers but occasionally there are pink varieties. I recently came across some with very pink flowers and dark purple stems. But the more common white flowered plants have green stems.

There is a succession in the flowering times of the different woodland umbellifers. First to flower in the woods is Cow Parsley, Pignut and Sanicle. Next is Hogweed which flowers in woods only about two weeks later, so there is some overlap. Ground Elder then enters the fray after a few weeks, so I suspect that many do not distinguish between Cow Parsley and Ground Elder. Both are white and have a frothy flamboyance in late spring. Later in the year comes Hemlock, and still later, Wild Angelica.

Hogweed, the pink variety

A word of warning about Hogweed: if the sap comes into contact with the skin it can cause it to blister, especially if the skin also gets a dose of sunshine, so one is at some risk if removing Hogweed from your own woodland path with a strimmer on a hot sunny day. There are many photographs of burns caused by Hogweed and although these are mostly caused by Giant Hogweed, Common Hogweed does also contain chemicals which can cause a rash and irritations.

This group of plants contains several noxious species, the most notorious of which is Hemlock whilst other species, such as Alexanders and Ground Elder are said to be edible. Hogweed has been used to make soup but it needs thorough cooking in order to remove toxic chemicals.

Many insects, particularly hoverflies, visit Hogweed for the nectar. In the photograph showing the pink version, many little insects can be seen crawling over the surface.

It has been suggested that the scientific name of the genus is derived from Hercules and may refer to the strength and robust nature of the plant or to some strength-giving virtues supposed to be possessed by it.

The green stems of Hogweed

The more common white flower specimen

Common Spotted Orchid

COMMON SPOTTED ORCHID

Dactylorhiza fuchsii

The Common Spotted Orchid is one of the most common orchids in Great Britain. Part of the reason for this is because it will grow in a variety of habitats, from fairly shady woodland through to open meadows and roadside verges.

In colour it can vary from almost white to pink and there are even some decidedly purple specimens. The flowers have dark spots and lines on them which are honey guides. The two main characteristics to aid with identification are the shape of the lip petal which is distinctly pointed and the leaves which are marked with dark purple spots or bars. This latter characteristic is also shared with the Early Purple Orchid and some Marsh Orchid species.

The Common Spotted Orchid could be confused with the Heath Spotted Orchid which favours the undergrowth of dry forests, but the latter has a much more rounded lip petal and the central pointed part is small and does not extend in a prominent way like the Common Spotted Orchid. The other possibility for confusion is with the various types of Marsh Orchid but their leaves are not generally distinctly spotted and the lip petal of the flower is rounded, without a central pointed area.

These orchids, unlike many other species, seem to have maintained their populations in recent times, although numbers fluctuate greatly in the same area, from year to year. There is a small meadow near to our own woodland where one year there must have been several hundred flowering. In the following year there were only about thirty. This fluctuation is often the case with orchids.

The Common Spotted Orchid flowers in late May to the end of June. They can reach a height of 70cm at a push. Flowering when they do means that they are unlikely to be confused with the Early Purple Orchid, which grows in ancient woodland, but by the end of May has flowered and will already have advanced seed pods.

Common Spotted Orchids in Ninewells Wood

COMMON TWAYBLADE

Listera ovata

Common Twayblade

Common Twayblade is an orchid but it could not be further from the preconceived exotic glamour of the species. Even compared to most British orchids, it is far from exciting to look at. However it is an orchid and as such has the typical orchid flower structure of three sepals and three petals.

The sepals are fairly straightforward. One protrudes and two are diagonally down to the right and to the left. The petals are arranged so that two to the left and right look like normal petals, and a third petal which is central, is modified into a sort of tube, comprising a column and a lip. It is within this part of the flower that the male and female reproductive structures are located.

Twayblade is sometimes referred to as the Green Man Orchid because of its appearance but it still has the basic orchid pattern. It is probably the most common orchid in Britain and is found in a variety of habitats including woodland, although it has declined nationwide in recent years due largely to ancient meadows being 'improved' or removed.

It has two big round leaves which are arranged opposite one another, hence the name Twayblade. It flowers from mid-May to June. The flowers are pollinated by a wide range of insects but particularly by parasitic wasps, sawflies and beetles. The pollinia (modified anthers which form the male part) lie free on top of the gutter-shaped rostellum which is at the centre of the flower. This organ is filled with a viscous fluid. When an insect touches the sensitive tip of the rostellum, this fluid is ejected and glues the pollinia to the visitor's body. When this insect then visits another flower, the pollinia touch the stigma and pollination takes place. In the case of Twayblade a wide variety of insects can fulfil this role and the production of seed is consequently successful.

NAVELWORT
Umbilicus rupestris

This plant is shade tolerant, and can be found growing out of walls which enclose woodlands. It is also known as Wall Pennywort. The name relates to the leaf's resemblance to a belly button.

The leaves of this plant are edible and are highly regarded by foragers and chefs. I first became aware of this when I visited Whitebrook Restaurant in the Wye Valley, a Michelin-starred establishment which uses locally sourced wild herbs, including Pennywort, Three Cornered Garlic, Bittercress, Wild onion, Hogweed and Lesser Celandine. The Pennywort leaves were succulent and refreshing. The young leaves are quite thick and have a slightly spongy texture which holds in the juices which are a little tangy and at the same time mildly sweet.

If one should be tempted to pick a few leaves to add to one's bacon sandwich, then care needs to be taken when removing them from the parent plant, as it would be easy to pull the entire plant out from the wall in which it is growing.

It is in the same family as the Stonecrops Crassulaceae which also grow on walls and rocky places. Navelwort flowers grow tall into a spike and are more impressive than those of the other Stonecrops. The colour can vary from creamy off-white through to pink. They normally flower in May or June.

As the flower spike is just coming into bloom, the leaves are already starting to go over. At this stage some of the leaves have yellow and orange shades and perhaps they look less appetising. The best time to collect a few leaves to mix into a salad would be early in the year.

Navelwort in bud

Navelwort in flower, with last year's seed head on right

WOOD VETCH

Vicia sylvatica

Wood vetch

Wood Vetch has stunning flowers which are large for the vetch group, and it is shade tolerant, enjoying scrambling over dead trees in a woodland.

I found Wood Vetch when it was not in flower, but there were large dark green clumps of it. The leaves were made up of small clusters and each leaflet had a little spine at its end and a tendril which branched out at the tip. These were all good indications that it was Wood Vetch.

This was in April and I returned to the site at the beginning of June, by which time the plants had developed into impressive mounds. The stems seemed to have piled up on one another. There was nothing in the immediate vicinity for them to climb up, which is what I suspect they would have done if some woodland shrubs had been growing close by. A few were flowering but most were in bud. The ones receiving most light were in bloom. The ones further back would be in bloom within a few weeks.

At first sight the flowers appear white but on closer inspection subtle shades of light blue can be identified along with blue-to-purple lines running down through the main upright petals, making them quite beautiful.

This is a lovely perennial plant in woodlands and seeds and potted Wood Vetch plants are available from a few garden centres for those who want it in their gardens. With its shade-tolerance and ability to climb up or scramble over rocks and dead trees, it is ideal for difficult areas of a garden.

Seed head

HERB BENNET
Geum urbanum

Herb Bennet, also known as Wood Avens and St Benedict's Herb, is prolific in wood or anywhere shady, but it can be overlooked as it flowers at the same time as the Buttercup and often in close proximity to it, so at a casual glance all that can be seen are small yellow flowers. Even the leaf of Herb Bennet is similar to a Buttercup leaf. The flowering period is long, from May through to August. It is not related to the Buttercup but is part of the rose family.

It has two culinary uses. The root tastes of cloves and is best picked, washed and dried as the clove taste grows in intensity after drying. The leaves can also be picked and deep fried whereupon they puff up like prawn crackers. In days gone by the roots were hung up by the door so that the smell of cloves would ward off evil spirits.

The seed head is made up of a bunch of single seeds, each of which has a long spike with a little hook on the end, so

Herb Bennet flower

its dispersal mechanism is via animals with the hooked seed getting caught their fur or indeed on the trousers or socks of humans.

There is a similar plant, Water Avens, which has larger apricot-coloured flowers. This will also grow in wet woodland and if there is any Wood Avens nearby, then it will hybridise with it. This results in a complete range of colours of flowers, from pure yellow through lots of intermediate colour to the apricot of the Water Avens.

The name St Benedict's Herb could be a corruption of 'blessed herb' or it may be connected with Saint Benedict, as it was believed to ward off evil spirits.

GREATER BIRDSFOOT TREFOIL
Lotus pedunculatus

The main difference between Greater Birdsfoot Trefoil and Common Birdsfoot Trefoil, is that the former has more flowers per head, between 5-12, and the flowers are pure yellow, whereas Common Birdsfoot Trefoil only has 3-6 flowers and these can include some orange which gives rise to its other common name of 'eggs and bacon'.

The 'birdsfoot' name comes from the arrangement of the seed pods which splay out like a bird's foot. The word 'trefoil' is a reference to the leaves which are composed of three leaflets.

The Greater Birdsfoot Trefoil has hollow stems and the leaves are a richer green. It grows in damp and sometimes shady woodland habitats, whereas Common Birdsfoot Trefoil prefers drier and more open habitats such as an airy glade.

They are both members of the Leguminosae or Pea family and as such have root nodules which can fix nitrogen.

As a result they can live in areas where the supply of nitrates is inadequate for other species. Common Birdsfoot Trefoil can live on sand dunes and very poor woodland soil.

Greater Birdsfoot Trefoil

Young Caper Spurge on woodland path

CAPER SPURGE

Euphorbia lathyris

Caper Spurge grows as a native plant in woods but is more often a garden weed than a wild flower. Caper Spurge produces a white viscous liquid when damaged which is very caustic, causing burning of the skin and severe damage if it gets into the eyes. The Caper Spurge is said via this to keep moles at bay.

The seed pods resemble capers, as do the seeds of Nasturtiums, but whereas the Nasturtiums can be eaten and make a good substitute for capers, the Caper Spurge is poisonous. The pods swell up and eventually achieve a size larger than a caper, then they burst and scatter the seeds.

In Britain it has a scattered distribution, with Hertfordshire and London favoured, along with a few others areas along the English/Welsh border. It has a mixed presence elsewhere and shows a marked decrease further north.

Bracts and tiny flowers

CREEPING JENNY
Lysimachia nummularia

Creeping Jenny

reeping Jenny is a perennial, low-growing plant and is a member of the Primulaceae family, being most closely related to the Loosestrifes. It can be found in wet woodland, pond margins and boggy areas. Its closest relative is Yellow Pimpernel which is very similar but is smaller and more delicate.

The leaves of Yellow Pimpernel are more pointed and in Creeping Jenny they are more heart-shaped. Also, the five individual petals of Yellow Pimpernel are separate whereas in Creeping Jenny they are larger, more robust and overlap one another. Yellow Pimpernel starts to flower in March or April and Creeping Jenny does not really get going until May. It is common in Wales and Southern England.

Creeping Jenny with pollinating insects

MONKSHOOD

Aconitum napellus

Monkshood, the cultivated variety

This is a native species. Monkshood is very poisonous, causing the rapid onset of life-threatening heart rhythm changes along with possible numbness and tingling, nausea, vomiting, abdominal pain and diarrhoea. Respiratory paralysis and heart rhythm abnormalities can rapidly lead to death and there is no specific antidote! Ingestion, and even touch, can be lethal.

I have only seen one Monkshood specimen growing in the wild. It grows in the shade and can be found in woodland, although it is rare and is often a garden escapee. There are many varieties of Monkshood, with variations in the colour and shape of the flower.

The wild variety has a low profile to the hood, whereas in some of the garden varieties, the hood is quite developed and looks more like a helmet than a hood. The one photographed on the left closely resembles the wild variety although it was in fact cultivated.

Monkshood pollen has been found during pollen analysis of ancient peat cores. However most of the Monkshood plants now growing in Britain are believed to be of garden origin and these are usually not *A. napellus,* but a hybrid with the closely-related southern European species *A. variegatum.* The cross is called *A. x cammarum*, Hybrid (or Garden) Monkshood. Generally, a native population will comprise a large colony of thousands of plants whereas garden escapes are more likely to be found as single plants or just a very few individuals.

A similar and related plant is Wolfsbane which has the same shaped flowers but they are smaller and a creamy yellow. Wolfsbane can also be found in woodlands in the wild, as an escapee.

Monkshood growing wild, but quite possibly a garden escapee

WHITE, NARROW-LEAVED and RED HELLEBORINE

Cephalanthera damasonium, Cephalanthera longifolia and Cephalanthera rubra

Helleborines are a sub-group of the wider group of the Orchids.

None of the three Helleborines listed here are common, but the one that is the least rare is the White Helleborine *Cephalanthera damasonium*. This flowers early, in alkaline, chalky or limestone areas, sometimes associated with Beech woodland. According to the BSBI it can be found in 233 hectads in the UK. Most of these are in southern central areas of England, where the terrain is chalky or limestone.

Narrow-leaved Helleborine *Cephalanthera longifolia* is also known as Sword-leaved Helleborine. It too favours alkaline soils and is even more rare, but it does have a more widespread distribution, being found in the north of Britain, particularly north-western Scotland, as opposed to the almost exclusively southern distribution of the White Helleborine. It is only found in only 131 hectads in Britain and 31 in Ireland.

The Narrow-leaved Helleborine in the photo was growing on the edge of Beech woods above Stroud in the Cotswolds. There were just two groups, one consisting of two spikes which were well past flowering and were developing their seed pods

White Helleborine

White Helleborine

Narrow-leaved Helleborine

in mid-May, and a second group with three spikes which were flowering well.

Finally, the star of this show is the Red Helleborine, *Cephalanthera rubra*, which is not red but is a fantastic pink to purple colour, an absolutely stunning orchid. It is also the rarest of these three, being found in only ten hectads in Britain and as such in the Critically Endangered category in Britain. It often fails to flower for several consecutive years, and is not easy to spot.

However, it is more common in Europe and I have been privileged to see it growing in coastal woodlands in France, although it is more likely to be found in south-eastern regions of the country.

Red Helleborine

Red Helleborine

SPREADING BELLFLOWER

Campanula patula

Spreading Bellflower

Spreading Bellflower is an attractive, delicate wild plant of the woodlands with a lot of little Harebell-like flowers. This Bellflower grows with several upright stalks which then spread out, whereas the Nettle-leaved Bellflower has just one stalk.

Both are woodland plants but will grow quite happily in the hedgerows in full sunshine. It is not particularly common in Britain which is at the northern extreme of its global distribution. In France it is more common, growing in deciduous and pine forests, woods, fields and roadsides, along railway lines and hedgerows, preferably in partial shade, in dry-to-moist sites and on clay soils, relatively rich in nitrogen.

The Creeping Bellflower *Campanula rapunculoides* is related to it. This is more commonly found as a garden plant but escapes do occur so it might also be seen in the countryside. It can be distinguished from Spreading Bellflower in that the splits between the petals are less deep. Those of the Spreading Bellflower cut back into the bell by more than half the length. The individual bells of Spreading Bellflower grow at right angles to the stem or even point upwards, whilst the bells of Creeping Bellflower hang down.

SLENDER
St JOHN'S WORT

Hypericum pulchrum

There are several species of St. John's Wort growing in Britain, all quite similar and it is the presence or absence of tiny black dots on the edges of the petals and the sepals and sometimes the leaves which is the key to their identification.

Six species of St. John's Wort grow in woodland: Pale St. John's Wort and Imperforate (*see page 180*); Slender St. John's Wort; Trailing St. Johns Wort; Upright St John's Wort; and Tutsan (*see page 147*).

Slender St. John's Wort is probably the most attractive, as the petals are a rich yellow with orange almost red colouring underneath, so when some of the flowers are in bloom and some in bud there is an attractive red, orange, and yellow display. The petals are edged with red and with black dots and the sepals are edged with black dots. The leaves too have little translucent dots spread randomly over their surface.

The flowers appear in June and are over by July, when just the seed capsules remain.

This species grows in open woodland but it is also to be found on heathland and in scrub areas.

Slender St. John's Wort is commonly used in herbal remedies. It is supposed to relieve depression, and is commercially marketed as a remedy. It contains the chemicals hypericin and hyperfolin, both of which owe their names to the scientific name for St. John's Worts.

St. John's Wort was named after St. John the Baptist as the spots on its petals represent the spots of blood which fell at his beheading. The translucent spots on the leaves were said to be the tears wept for him on his death.

Slender St John's Wort

Wall Lettuce flowers

WALL LETTUCE
Mycelis muralis

Wall Lettuce is related to the lettuce we eat in salads but it is not in the same genus. It is closely related to the Chicory genus. The flowers of all these species are similar and the leaves edible. Wall Lettuce has yellow flowers. It may be surprising to learn that a lettuce produces flowers but if it did not then there would be no packets of lettuce seeds in the garden centre. If one fails to harvest lettuce from the garden, especially in a hot, dry summer, it bolts and produces a tall stem topped with lots of little yellow flowers which look similar to those of the Wall Lettuce. In the case of Wall Lettuce, the flowers have only five petals and the central region is made up of stamens and stigmas so there are no actual disc florets. The Sunflower, on the other hand has hundreds of disc florets making up the central 'face' of the flower. The Wall Lettuce is probably the simplest form of composite flower.

Wall Lettuce are quite at home in woodlands and tolerate dry conditions. The leaves are similar to the leaves of Fat Hen.

It is a perennial but fairly short-lived. Although its flowers are small, they produce vast numbers of light, feathery seeds which soon find a nice moist spot.

The flowers of the Wall Lettuce are very small and widely spaced which makes photographing them more difficult. The random spacing means if one is in focus, the chances are that the rest will not be. Moreover, because the flower stalk can grow to two metres, then if there is the slightest hint of a breeze, the flowers rock about all over the place, resulting in blurry photographs.

IVY BROOMRAPE

Orobanche hederae

Ivy Broomrape

There are many species of Broomrape and they are all parasitic. Ivy Broomrape lives on Ivy. Its roots form a union with the Ivy roots and draw water and nutrients from it and so Broomrape does not have any chlorophyll, therefore no green pigment. It has rudimentary leaves up the stem which are light brown in colour.

It is a rare plant. Because it grows on Ivy it can be found in woodlands, especially those near the coast if they are rocky and fairly open.

Other Broomrapes found in Britain include Common Broomrape, Knapweed Broomrape, Thyme Broomrape, Thistle Broomrape and Bedstraw Broomrape. In Europe there are many more. It flowers from late May to July.

Ivy Broomrape growing amongst its host Ivy plants

FOXGLOVE
Digitalis purpurea

I had a lot of Foxgloves growing in my area of woodland for a while. This was not surprising as this is one of the first wild flowers to colonise an area of woodland when it has been felled. There were a few to be found around the edge of my wood before the Corsican Pines were removed but after the felling they appeared throughout the area, not just around the perimeter. In a few years the numbers started to decline as the Silver Birch and other deciduous trees grew up and the light levels subsided again.

Foxglove seeds are programmed to germinate only in light conditions. A single plant can produce over 7,000 seeds, so it is not surprising that lots of plants pop up after a wood has been cleared. How long the seeds remain viable in the soil is an interesting question. There are numerous estimates, varying from five years to several decades, but there is no unanimity on the point. My view is that some seeds may remain viable for as long as 50 years. I base this on the fact that my Corsican Pines were about 55 years old when cut, so the wood had been subject

Foxgloves at Ninewells Wood

to deep shade for a period of 50 years. After the pines had been removed and the brash had been gathered, the newly exposed soil quickly produced the new Foxglove plants.

I try to maintain a mix of densities in my regenerating woodland; and a variety of species of trees to produce varying amounts of light at ground level, so something will favour the continued growth of Foxgloves.

Foxgloves flower in their second year. They then usually survive to produce flowers in their third and fourth years and in these later years the flower spike is not as large. The colours can be a variety of shades of purple, and even white versions can sometimes occur.

It is a well-known fact that this plant is poisonous but the chemicals it contains, when extracted and administered in the right dosage, can be very effective in treating heart failure. A product called digoxin was approved for the treatment of heart failure in 1998. One should definitely not be tempted into any form of self-administration however. It could kill you.

Although it is toxic to us, it is the food plant for the Lesser Yellow Underwing Moth and another moth called the Foxglove Pug *Eupithecia pulchellata*.

The caterpillar of Lesser Yellow Underwing will eat a variety of other plants but the Foxglove Pug is more fussy and has an interesting survival technique. Once it hatches, it selects a Foxglove flower and using sticky silk threads it seals the opening of the tubular flower and proceeds to eat the reproductive parts, the anthers and stigmas, eventually pupating inside the flower.

Flowers which have a resident Foxglove Pug will remain on the flower stalk long after others, which were not selected, have withered and died.

Foxglove flowerhead

SKULLCAP
Scutellaria sp.

Lesser Skullcap

There are three species of Skullcap which grow in Britain but the one called Somerset Skullcap is incredibly rare and only grows in a couple of locations, so I will only deal with the other two and even these are not particularly common.

The less scarce of the two is simply known as Skullcap *Scutellaria galericulata*, sometimes called Common Skullcap, Marsh Skullcap or even Hooded Skullcap. I recently came across some in woods in Worcestershire, where the Skullcap was growing in a wet ditch at the side of a woodland path.

Skullcap flowers from June to September and it has a typical Labiate shape of flower, similar to Bugle except that the flowers are normally produced in pairs at each node whereas with Bugle there is normally a ring of about six or so pointing out in every direction. The flowers are a similar blue colour.

It is a low creeping or spreading plant usually found in wet areas along the edge of ponds and ditches. It is tolerant of shade so is also found in woodlands. Predominantly it is found in the central regions of Britain and becomes less common on the east and west coast.

The name Skullcap comes from the scientific name *scutella* meaning a small dish. The flower shape, if inverted, bears a vague resemblance to a small dish. It is used in traditional herbal medicines for a variety of ailments including rabies.

The other species of Skullcap is Lesser Skullcap *Scutellaria minor* which is perhaps more often found in woodlands, especially where there has been open cast coal mining nearby. I visit many areas in the Forest of Dean, several of them now quite beautiful, and rich in wildlife – in complete contrast to the industrial sites they were 50 years ago. Recently I came across both species of Skullcap growing in such an area. Lesser and Common Skullcap will also hybridise. The pure Lesser Skullcap has pink flowers as opposed to the blue of the common species.

Common Skullcap

TUTSAN
Hypericum androsaemum

Tutsan flowers

Tutsan is one of the St. John's wort family and is native to Britain. Because many people grow it in the garden, it is also spread into the countryside when birds eat and disperse the fruits and therefore the seeds.

Tutsan seems an odd name, but is a compound of *tout saine*, French words meaning 'all healthy", surely a reference to its healing properties. Lots of our plant names have a French origin, courtesy of William the Conqueror. In his 1653 publication *Culpepper's Complete Herbal,* Nicholas Culpepper states that '*Tutsan purgeth choleric humours...both to cure sciatica and gout, and to heal burnings by fire.*' The berries which turn from white to green to red and then to black are, however poisonous.

There is a clue to its healing properties in its scientific name, *Hypericum*, which is the genus that contains all the St Johns Worts, one of the mainstays of herbalists and alternative medicine practitioners.

The plant is really a small bush growing to a height of about 1.5m. It grows in shady places. I have found it on the edge of woodland paths and in woodland glades. It flowers in June and July. The flowers are bright and showy, with five golden yellow petals and a big star burst bunch of stamens in the centre, splaying outwards. Right in the centre is the shiny bold and blatantly feminine ovary. This will develop into the fruit. Initially it is green but it soon swells up and ripens.

Seed heads

WOOD DOCK

Rumex sanguineus

Wood Dock resembles 'normal' Dock but it is thinner and it thrives in the shady conditions of a woodland. There are in fact several species of Dock but there are just two 'normal' Docks, Broad-leaved Dock *Rumex obtusifolius* and Curled Dock *R. crispus,* both of which are common throughout Britain and as hybrids.

Wood Dock often grows in open glades in woodlands. The photograph on the right was taken just before it flowered so the flowers are still wrapped up in a sheath.

With the passing of the season, the flowers open out and it may develop red veins in the leaves which is the reason for its other common name, Red Veined Dock. The stems of this species are straight and upright and this is a diagnostic feature, as other Docks tend to have slightly 'zigzag' stems.

When I was teaching students ecology, Dock was one of the few plant names that the students knew, as a result of its ability to relieve pain from stinging nettles. Because they knew that once stung, one needed to find a Dock leaf, they would invariably refer to the plant as a 'Dock leaf' and I would invariably have to point out that it is just plain 'Dock'. Whether they remembered this, I doubt.

Wood Dock flowers

HEDGE WOUNDWORT

Stachys sylvatica

Hedge Woundwort

edge Woundwort is in the nettle family and has many of the group's characteristic features including the square stems with the flowers arranged in whorls up the stem and the individual flowers have the typical nettle appearance with a lower lip and a small tubular structure. The leaves are nettle-like but do not sting and are soft and furry. If the leaves are touched or crushed they have a powerful and unpleasant smell. This could be this plant's means of deterring browsing animals from eating it.

The flowers of the Hedge Woundwort are a dark purple-red, sometimes described as beetroot red. There are other woundworts but generally their flowers are a much lighter shade of pink. Red Dead Nettle has similar coloured flowers to the Hedge Woundwort but is a much smaller plant and its flowers are bunched up, not in separate whorls. Hedge Woundwort grows up to 1m in height.

The leaf is very similar to other species in the family, although slightly less jagged. The smell is the best way to identify it. It is difficult to describe: I would say a mixture of plastic, smoke, burnt rubber and chemicals.

It is shade tolerant and I often come across it growing on the edge of woodland rides and paths. It starts to flower in June and continues throughout the summer.

As the name suggests, it has been used in the past as a herbal remedy, supposedly good at stopping bleeding.

Hedge Woundwort spike

WILD MADDER

Rubia peregrina

Wild Madder flower

Wild Madder is in the bedstraw family which includes Cleavers, and Woodruff. There are two species of Madder: Wild Madder, which is the one to be found in the woods; and Field Madder.

Symonds Yat is a good place to see Wild Madder as it grows all around the viewing point for the peregrine falcons. I doubt that many people looking across the Wye Valley from this vantage point trying to spot the peregrine falcons are likely to notice this plant at their feet, but it is there.

The genus name derives from the Latin *ruber* meaning 'red', as the roots of some species (mainly *Rubia tinctorum)* have been used since ancient times as red vegetable dye. The species name derives from the Latin adjective *peregrinus*, meaning 'foreign, an alien traveller, a pilgrim'.

As with all the plants in this group, the leaves are distinctive, arranged in whorls of 5-7 leaves at the joins (nodes) along the stem. The mature leaves of Madder are robust, shiny and with jagged edges. Several species in this group have leaves with rough or jagged edges which helps them grow up and gain purchase between other species and reach the light.

The leaves of this species remain throughout the winter so it is an evergreen plant. The stems are square and have little spines on the edges, also there to help them get a grip on whatever they are growing over. It will tolerate shade and woodland but will only grow where the soil pH is above seven. It is very much restricted to the west and south-west of Britain.

The flowers are small with four little creamy yellow petals arranged in a cross. Sometimes, if quite a few come into bloom at the same time, they can make a bit of a show.

It is the fruits which are most spectacular. They are large and spherical and when ripe they are dark blue, almost black, like a mini bunch of grapes.

Wild Madder fruits

GREATER BUTTERFLY ORCHID
Platanthera chlorantha

The Greater Butterfly Orchid is majestic but can be overlooked as it often grows where Bluebells have flowered. When the orchid comes into flower in late May or June, the Bluebells have gone over so the orchid, which is white or greenish white, gets obscured by the now fruiting Bluebell spears with their developing seed heads which are also greenish white at this time of year.

There are two Butterfly Orchids, Greater and Lesser, and they are very similar but the pollinia (specially modified anthers found on orchids) on the Greater Butterfly Orchid spread out to form an inverted 'V' shape whereas in the case of the Lesser Butterfly Orchid they hang down and are parallel to one another. Indeed the scientific name, *Planthera*, means spreading anthers. The pollinia turn brown as they get older.

The Greater Butterfly Orchid is the more common of the two and is found particularly in the central southern counties of England. They prefer alkaline soils. The BSBI cite its loss from many sites during the last century due to felling, disturbance and extensive conifer plantations along with agricultural improvement of pasture and scrub. They also suggest that it may be lost from woodland if the canopy becomes too dense.

It grows up to 60cm in height and has two or three large leaves at the base, but it also has a few little spear-shaped leaves up the flower spike. The flowers are loosely arranged and usually number about ten. They are white with green markings so in the deep shade of the woods they often look slightly green. The flower stalks which become the ovary have a peculiar spiral twisted look and the flower has a very long spur, suggesting that the Greater Butterfly Orchid is pollinated by insects with a correspondingly long tongue. The spur extends back well past the main flower stalk.

Greater Butterfly Orchid

Greater Butterfly Orchid

MARTAGON LILY
Lilium martagon

The Martagon Lily is a special flower, rare and beautiful. It is so called because the petals curve back and look a bit like the cap Turkish people once wore. In Ottoman Turkish, a *martagan* is both a kind of turban and the lily. Another name for it is Turk's Cap Lily. It is sold by many garden centres and is included in many herbaceous borders, where it is quite useful as it grows in the more shaded areas.

The general opinion is that it was introduced to Britain in the 14th century. There is certainly evidence that it had been introduced into British gardens by 1596. It was first recorded in the wild in 1782, and in 1883 in the Wye Valley, where it was once considered to be native in ancient woodland. There is little evidence of significant change in distribution since the BSBI 1962 Atlas.

It is recorded as being present in just two regions in the Wye Valley which include Tintern, Brockweir and Lippetts Grove. It is only recorded in 312 hectads in the whole of Britain and Ireland and these are mainly along the border between England and Scotland. Many of these recordings are plants which have originated from garden stock. Worldwide it grows all across Europe and into Asia as far as Mongolia, so whilst rare here, it is not threatened on a global scale. The plants in the Wye Valley are growing a long way from any habitation as my aching back will testify, having carried all my heavy camera gear to the site and back.

They grow to about one metre tall and have several flowers on each spike.

Martagon Lily showing stamens

Martagon Lilies have bulbs, in common with all lilies, which is how they overwinter. It is suggested that birds such as jays may dig up the bulbs and in that way aid distribution. As gardeners know, the bulb of a lily is quite a loose structure and individual swollen leaf bases will break off easily. Each one of these can potentially develop into a new plant so whilst the jay may eat some of the bulb, other bits will be distributed. Grey squirrels could well use Martagon Lilies as a food source and spread them in the same way.

The other method of propagation is by seed. The flowers develop into large seed pods containing heavy seeds which are flung from the pod when it is windy, but do not travel very far. Both methods of distribution rely on easy access to the soil, whereas a thick layer of brash reduces the chances of new plants being established.

I have seen another population of Martagon Lilies in some other local woods. Having stopped to admire a roe deer, I noticed some large pink flowers, four or five on each stalk, a little way off the path. I recognised them as Martagon Lilies and found that there were about 15 individuals all grouped in one fairly small region of the woods.

All parts of this plant are reputed to be extremely toxic to cats and it is advised that people who have a pet cat should not plant it in their garden. Even brushing past the flowers could result in pollen being deposited on the cat's fur, which when cleaned will cause it some distress or even death.

Martagon Lily flower spike

BITTERSWEET

Solanum dulcamara

Bittersweet: developing fruits

Bittersweet is also known as Woody Nightshade, and many people refer to it incorrectly as Deadly Nightshade, which it is not. They are related as they are both in the Solanaceae family and they are both poisonous, but the Deadly Nightshade has larger black fruits that are spherical whereas Bittersweet has smaller red fruits which are egg-shaped. The fruits of Bittersweet form in bunches, whereas Deadly Nightshade bears its fruits singly. Potatoes and tomatoes are also in this family and the flowers of Bittersweet bear a close resemblance to the flowers of these garden vegetables and fruits.

The fruits of the Bittersweet start off green and as they ripen they turn yellow and then red, and resemble a group of miniature plum tomatoes, but they are poisonous. They contain an alkaloid, solanine, which acts narcotically. In large doses it paralyses the central nervous system, without affecting the peripheral nerves or voluntary muscles. It slows the heart and respiration, lessens sensibility, lowers the temperature and causes vertigo and delirium, terminating in death with convulsions.

Bittersweet: flowers and fruits

This plant is a scrabbler, which is to say that it winds its way around other plants and up through bushes to gain height and light, almost vine-like in its growth. This is a strength when it comes to climbing up shrubs and trees in the woods to gain access to more light. It flowers throughout the summer and the fruits look attractive in the autumn.

Apart from Deadly Nightshade, *Atropa bella-donna*, there are other nightshades in the same genus such as Black Nightshade, *Solanum nigrum*. This is more likely to be found in cultivated ground, whereas Bittersweet is more likely to be found in open woodland or a hedgerow. There is also Green Nightshade and Hairy Nightshade.

Cicely Mary Barker (28 June 1895-16 February 1973) was an English illustrator best known for a series of fantasy illustrations depicting fairies and flowers. She depicted a fairy in the style of Bittersweet.

Bittersweet: close-up of flowers

COMMON GROMWELL

Lithospermum officinale

The full plant

Common Gromwell is a bushy plant growing to about one metre in height and it produces creamy green flowers.

It favours an alkaline soil with trees and shrubs dotted about in the grassland to provide some degree of shade. The seeds are quite distinctive shiny little grey-to-white nutlets.

The name Gromwell relates to these seeds. It comes from the French *grémil* a combination of two words 'gré' (grey, the colour) and 'mil' (for millet seed). Grey millet is the same colour as the nutlets. The seeds tend to be grey to start with and grow whiter as they mature. It was once believed that these little grey nutlets might contain a contraceptive substance.

Recently I came across a lot of these plants in the Forest of Dean growing along a track leading away from an area known as Speculation. The Forest of Dean was an area of iron and coal mining. Speculation was at one time a coal mine but little remains to indicate this today apart from the old railway tracks, now used by walkers and cyclists. It was along one of these tracks that the Common Gromwell was growing, its presence perhaps due to the fact that the soil along the old railway track is alkaline, as a result of the material used in the construction of the tracks to make up the substrate, possibly limestone chippings. Most forest soils are acidic. I found these plants in mid-September and most of them only had the little nutlet or seed showing. There were only a few which still had some flowers in bloom.

Common Gromwell is not actually very common; its distribution is constrained by its preference for alkaline soils.

There is another species called Purple Gromwell although it is actually more blue than purple and it too can be found in open woodland situations and hedgerows.

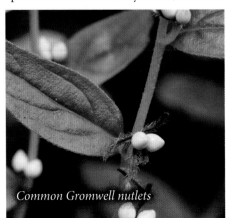
Common Gromwell nutlets

Common Gromwell flower

STINKING IRIS

Iris foetidissima

Stinking Iris

The first thing to note is that Stinking Iris does not stink. It does have a smell but only if the leaves are crushed and it is not as offensive a smell as that of many other flowers such as the American Skunk Cabbage which can be smelt at some distance from where the plants are growing. Some flowers have an unpleasant smell in order to attract pollinators in the form of flies which think it is a dead animal. In fact many plants smell when their leaves are bruised. Elder, for example, has a really unpleasant smell when crushed.

The smell of Stinking Iris is said to be reminiscent of roast beef although I do not find it so. The flower has a typical iris design with three sections. It is a pale cream blending into a pinkish purple and although not as attractive as the Yellow Flag Iris, when freshly in bloom it does have its subtleties.

The photograph was taken in late June. The flowering season extends from late May until at least July. However, when I first visited the area in early June, it was well off flowering. The buds had not even pushed their way out from between the leaves. The only indication that they would eventually produce flowers was a slight swelling lower down the leaf area. Several visits later, my efforts were rewarded. After flowering, Stinking Iris produces very attractive red berries which, in my opinion, out-perform the flowers.

It is a native species, tolerant of shade and of wet conditions and also grows in hedge banks. It is not evenly distributed, and is more commonly found in southern and western areas of Britain, although it is also fairly common in Suffolk. In some of the older wild flower and nature books I have seen it referred to as Gladdon and Stinking Gladwin.

BIRD'S NEST ORCHID

Neottia nidus-avis

Bird's Nest Orchid is a little gem of a flower, and I would like to thank Frank D Williams, a local naturalist for alerting me to this flower and helping me find it. This specimen was growing beside an old railway track, possibly because the limestone chippings used in the construction had rendered the soil alkaline. It had a grasshopper nymph on the top of the spike!

The first thing to note about this orchid is the colour, or lack of it. In particular there is no green colouration and therefore no chlorophyll. In order to survive, it needs to have a complicated relationship with a fungus. The fungus involved is called Sebacina, which in turn has a symbiotic relationship with certain trees, particularly Beech trees. The fungus network combines with the tree's roots, forming a mycorrhizal

Large group of Bird's Nest Orchids

relationship, deriving benefit in the form of sugars and other complex nutrients from the tree. The tree benefits from the fungus in that the fine threads of the fungus penetrate the soil and increase the capacity of the tree's roots to absorb minerals.

The Bird's Nest Orchid effectively gatecrashes this partnership so that its roots combine with the fungal mycorrhiza on the tree's roots and it takes in nutrients and water from the tree, but gives nothing back in return and so is a parasite.

It has rudimentary leaves which are a buff yellow as is the stalk. In fact Bird's Nest Orchids do have a very small amount of chlorophyll, but not enough to be visible and to give it green colour nor to carry out photosynthesis to produce sugars. Most orchids have a symbiotic relationship with soil fungi but this one has taken it a stage further and become totally parasitic.

I have gone from never having seen a Bird's Nest Orchid in the UK, to seeing them in several locations including one where there were 50–60 of them growing together in a loosely scattered patch.

It is called Bird's Nest orchid because, were one to dig it up, which of course would be totally illegal, one would find that the roots are matted together like a birds' nest. The word orchid comes from the Greek word orkhis meaning testicles because some orchids have roots which resemble a pair of testicles.

WOOD CRANESBILL

Geranium sylvaticum

Wood Cranesbill is a northern woodland plant, rarely found south of a line drawn from Manchester to Middlesborough.

Despite its name, it is found in a variety of habitats, woodland being one: also hay meadows, roadside banks and rocky ledges in the mountains. Having failed to see it in Scotland at the right time of year at the end of June, we took a detour via Cumbria on the little road from Kirkby Stephen: the B6270 is an absolute delight and to further add to its charms, it has Wood Cranesbill growing at the side of the road.

Wood Cranesbill

Flowers of Wood Cranesbill

YELLOW BIRD'S NEST

Monotropa hypopitys

Showing scale leaves

Yellow Bird's Nest is an unusual and fairly rare plant, recorded in 103 hectads. It is a parasite, or saprophyte, and has no chlorophyll so it looks white when it first appears and becomes increasingly brown as it ages. It does not have proper leaves, just scale leaves up its stem. The plants Toothwort and Bird's Nest Orchid look similar, and do not have chlorophyll either, but are unrelated.

Its distribution is scattered and it is rare north of Manchester. There are a few records of it in the Scottish lowlands and also in Ireland but it is a plant mainly of the south.

I have seen only these plants growing in ancient woodland largely composed of beech with a good understorey of hazel. I first came across the Yellow Bird's Nest fairly late in the summer and was not exactly sure what I was seeing as they were dark brown and withered at that stage so I thought that they might have been a Broomrape. The following year I was

Yellow Bird's Nest

visiting the same woods in mid-September when they were again very brown and dried up. I counted 21 individuals in one patch and found a second smaller group of four nearby.

Finally the year after that I visited at the right time of year, in June, and found a lot growing not just where I had first seen them but at several other locations nearby, probably adding up to over 200 individuals.

Recent research shows that it is epiparasitic, using a tricholoma fungus to extract nutrients from living trees in its vicinity and Beech or Hazel seem to be the most popular.

HIGH SUMMER

(JULY AND AUGUST)

Rosebay Willowherb

This is a great time of year not only for woodland flowers, but also for all the insects, especially the butterflies, which feed on them. If one can find an open woodland glade rich with Marsh Thistle, Willowherbs, Meadowsweet, Common Valerian and the first of the Hemp Agrimony, then one could be in for a butterfly feast, and that is exactly what they are doing, feasting. They love frothy open-topped umbels where they can land easily and then work their way round, probing each little flower to extract a tiny sip of nectar. Butterflies, including the Red Admirals, Peacocks, Tortoiseshells and Commas, abound and some years they are joined by an influx of migratory Painted Ladies. Also visiting will be the diminutive Skippers, Speckled Woods, Gatekeepers and several Browns. Best of all is the Silver-washed Fritillary with its dramatic courtship flight.

Many of the woodland wild flowers will now be over and their life cycle will be moving into seed production. Interesting to look out for the different modes of seed dispersal. Woodland animals and birds are employed in this important task. The two basic techniques used are food or hooks. Many woodland plants produce bright, succulent berries that can be as attractive as the flowers and often more so. I am thinking of Black Bryony and White Bryony: neither have beautiful flowers, but the fruits would cause one to pause. The same can be said for Lords and Ladies and Tutsan. The other technique for seed dispersal is to hitch a ride on the fur or feathers of birds and animals with a hooked or sticky seed. I suppose the berries are in effect also hitching a ride through the gut of a bird or mammal, to be deposited some distance from the parent plant. Some of the hooked seeds can be attractive especially in the case of Herb Bennet or Wood Avens, the closely related Water Avens and even Burdock.

BROAD-LEAVED and VIOLET HELLEBORINE

Epipactis helleborine and Epipactis purpurata

The Helleborines are a branch of the Orchid family. The Broad-leaved Helleborine grows in woodlands and as the name suggests, this species has wide leaves, especially the lowest leaf which is more or less circular. Further up the stem, the leaves become longer and thinner and are arranged in a spiral around the stem. This is important because the Narrow-lipped Helleborine has similar flowers but its leaves are arranged in two opposite rows up the stem. The Violet Helleborine is another species which could cause confusion. The Violet Helleborine also has a spiral leaf arrangement but the green parts are usually from light to dark violet. The flowers of all these orchids are beautiful and complex, especially when

Broad-leaved Helleborine

viewed individually. The Broad-Leaved Helleborine has just one pollinia, which is visible in the centre of the flower and is bright white. Many orchids by contrast have two pollinia. The pollinia, where the pollen is located, becomes detached from the flower and stuck to the head of an insect thereby getting moved from one flower to another and so cross pollination occurs.

In the case of the Broad-leaved Helleborine, the insect vector is a wasp. The wasps visit the flowers to drink the nectar, which is the dark brown material immediately below the pollinia. Quite often this nectar has become fermented and is rich in alcohol. This results in the wasps becoming somewhat intoxicated and sometimes after visiting several flowers they fall in a drunken stupor.

Between the pollinia and the nectar is an off-white, light cream area called the 'viscidium' which is, as its name suggests, sticky and it ruptures when the wasp visits and sticks the pollinia to the wasp's head. This orchid has a complex and varied parasitic relationship with different fungi in the soil, possibly the truffle fungi. It may also be a partial parasite on some trees. All this is very clever but sometimes too clever for its own good. Over-specialisation and too much reliance on other specific species can backfire, especially if that other species declines or disappears.

The flower colours vary from almost red or purple to cream.

The Violet Helleborine is much more rare and is found mainly in south-east England, also in Herefordshire and Shropshire. It flowers from mid July through to September, peaking in early August. It likes Beech or Hornbeam woodland and can be found alongside woodland paths but it will also pop up deep in the woods in quite shady areas.

The Violet Helleborine has pale green flowers, not violet or purple as the name suggests. It is the leaves, and particularly the stem, which take up the violet colour.

Violet Helleborine

Wood Sage

WOOD SAGE

Teucrium scorodonia

Wood Sage is a common species in open woodland. It looks like the culinary herb sage and has a smell somewhere between lemons and cat's pee.

Thetford Forest where I took students on field studies, was largely Corsican Pine but there was an area where the Forestry Commission had planted some experimental blocks of different tree species. Some of the tree species filtered out a huge amount of light and as a result very little grew underneath them. Wood Sage was only found growing with tree species that allowed more light through to the forest floor, such as Hybrid Larch and Southern Beech.

We would measure the light with light meters and take soil samples, which were used to test pH and water content. The pH was always acidic there, whatever the type of tree, varying between 4.5-5. Water content did vary but the soil was generally dry.

Wood Sage lives in open woodland, favours an acid soil and will tolerate fairly dry soil. It is a perennial which flowers in mid summer. The flowers are not spectacular. They are arranged in a terminal spike and are a creamy, slightly greenish white. The petals are shaped in the typical nettle (labiate) arrangement. The stamens and anthers grow beyond the petals prominently and are purple.

The genus *Teucrium* is commonly known as Germander and includes species such as Wall Germander, Cut-leaved Germander and Water Germander but not Germander Speedwell which is in a completely different group.

Wood Sage has been used in all sorts of remedies, many associated with the skin. It was also used in beer-making. It is reputed to cause hallucinations and makes the beer green! It is believed to clear beer faster than hops. It went out of favour when glass beer mugs started to replace pewter as then the colour of the beer became more obvious.

With the recent popularity of craft beers and the inclusion of multiple ingredients, I wonder if Wood Sage has ever been incorporated in artisanal brews.

Wood Sage

HEDGE PARSLEY

Torilis japonica

Hedge Parsley leaf

Hedge Parsley, sometimes known by the name Upright Hedge Parsley, is a small umbellifer that might be mistaken for a rather tatty specimen of Cow Parsley. It flowers later than Cow Parsley, usually from late June to August, by which time Cow Parsley has finished flowering completely. It is a much smaller plant, and a little bit straggly, despite being called Upright.

It is often found in open woodland rides; it tolerates some but not deep shade so is happier in a hedgerow than dense woodland. The seed heads are distinctive with rough hooked seeds which are more or less circular and often purple. Their leaves are like those of Cow Parsley but hairier.

Hedge Parsley flowers

Marsh Thistle

MARSH THISTLE

Cirsium palustre

The Marsh Thistle is tolerant of shade and so, despite its name, it is often found in woods along paths and fire breaks. It prefers damp soil. It also grows outside woodlands as well, in wet meadows, moorlands and roadsides. It can reach heights over 2 metres.

The flowers are small and usually a deep purple, but can be white or pink, and are produced between June and October.

It is a statuesque plant with few short side branches. The stem is adorned with spiny wings and both these and the leaves can develop a purple tinge.

The flowers are much visited by insects as they are rich in nectar. They are particularly favoured by the Five Spot Burnett moth and several different species of butterfly such as the Red Admiral butterfly seen in the photograph.

Marsh Thistle visited by Red Admiral

COMMON WINTERGREEN *and* ROUND-LEAVED

Pyrola minor

Pyrola rotundifolia

There are several species of Wintergreen: Common Wintergreen, Intermediate Wintergreen, Round-leaved Wintergreen, Serrated Wintergreen and One-flowered Wintergreen. The ones I saw when I lived in Spain many years ago were One-flowered Wintergreen. All species are found in woodlands, particularly in pine woods.

They are relatively rare and most are restricted to the north of England and Scotland. Round-leaved Wintergreen is not only found in woodlands but also sometimes on sand dunes, especially if these have become overgrown with shrubs and trees, thus providing the shady conditions they favour. A few of the species have small southern populations, for example along the southern parts of the English-Welsh border.

Common Wintergreen flowers from June to August and is the only Wintergreen which has a slight hint of pink. All the others are white and have yellow stamens in the centre and a prominent stigma.

The photograph on the left of Common Wintergreen was taken in the Moray area of Scotland by Ian Green. As can be seen he is blessed with hundreds, probably thousands, growing in a small wood close to where he lives.

Common Wintergreen

Round-leaved Wintergreen

MEADOWSWEET

Filipendula ulmaria

I think that Meadowsweet is possibly the whitest flower to be found. There are lots of white flowers but many of them have a hint of cream or a touch of green or a slight pink blush, rather like those emulsion white paints which are white but not quite white. Meadowsweet is pure, brilliant white. The flower stems and stamens are yellow, and combined with the white flowers, especially when the flowers are going over and losing some of their petals, they could possibly appear cream, but the flowers themselves are white, very white.

I have seen it growing in profusion in the damp regions of

Meadowsweet

Developing seeds

Meadowsweet flowerheads

various woodlands, often in the years immediately following coppicing. It grows in the partial shade which is created by standard trees. I often also come across it growing in hedge banks where there is some degree of shade.

Superficially it looks like an umbellifer but it is in fact in the rose family. It t grows to about 150cm but occasionally can reach 200cm.

Meadowsweet has a wide range of uses. Some are medicinal, but it also imparts a nice smell when dried and was said to be Queen Elizabeth I's favourite herb for spreading on the floor to rid the air of unpleasant odours. It was also used in brewing, particularly mead.

It is claimed that it has properties similar to aspirin and a traditional recipe requires that one steeps 45 grams of dried flowers in one litre of near boiling water for ten minutes and then takes three cupfuls of the resulting potion each day between meals.

The seeds are interesting and attractive. They are green and have a pattern of little ridges on them, sometimes described as being like tiny clenched fists.

CENTAURY: COMMON and LESSER

Centaurium erythraea and C. pulchellum

The Centaury genus is very closely related to the Gentians and they do look quite similar, apart from the fact that they are pink and Gentians are blue.

I have seen the Common Centaury growing along woodland rides, roadside verges, in shady wooded areas and even on sand dunes and it is a mark of the versatility of wild flowers that they can grow ins such diverse habitats.

Lesser Centaury is much more scarce and has a fairly restricted distribution, mainly encountered in the south-east counties of England. There is also a rare species called Seaside Centaury and as one would expect it is found on the coast, largely restricted to those of north-west Britain. Both Common and Lesser Centaurys seem to favour neutral to alkaline, reasonably well-drained soils.

The flowers are more closely bunched together in the Common Centaury whereas the seed capsule behind the flower is much longer in the case of the Lesser Centaury. Both species are biennials, producing a little rosette of leaves in the first year, developing a strong tap root which stores food over the winter and then using this energy source in the second year to produce the flower spike and eventually the seeds.

The depth of the pink colour does vary. The shade seems to depend upon the amount of light they are receiving or lacking: those in deep woodland are a paler pink.

Common Centaury

WILLOWHERBS

Epilobium

PALE WILLOWHERB, AMERICAN WILLOWHERB AND BROAD-LEAVED WILLOWHERB

The Willowherbs (*Epilobium* sp.) are a bit of a nightmare to identify. There are twelve species in total growing in Britain, but only five of them are woodland species:

Pale Willowherb is the one species found exclusively in woodland. It is not common and is sometimes overlooked because of its unimpressive appearance. In common with American Willowherb, it has a square stem, but the flowers of the Pale Willowherb are slightly paler. The main characteristic that separates the two species is the presence or absence of a leaf stalk (petiole). The leaves of the American Willowherb do not have stalks and are attached directly to the main stem, whereas Pale Willowherb leaves have quite long stalks. The American Willowherb has red stems while those of the Pale Willowherb are the usual green. Just to confuse the issue, there are other Willowherbs with red stems including the Broad-leaved Willowherb.

American Willowherb (*Epilobium ciliatum*), as you might expect, comes from America. It has been recorded in Britain since 1930, initially thriving in south-east England but spreading rapidly to the north and west. It is a perennial herb which is found on disturbed ground, in felled woodland and waste ground. It disperses readily by seed, often colonising newly disturbed sites.

Broad-leaved Willowherb (*Epilobium montanum*). Despite its name, the leaves of Broad-leaved Willowherb are only slightly wider than those of the other Willowherbs. It spreads through seed dispersal and once established it can also spread with horizontally-growing rhizomes, forming a little patch. It is perennial and tenacious. It grows to about 70cm in height and produces a small number of pink flowers. It is a plant which will tolerate some shade and is therefore to be found in woodland glades and edges. This species has a round stem and apart from Hoary Willowherb which rarely occurs in woodland, it is the only woodland species to show this characteristic. It is fairly common but, unlike American Willowherb, this species is native to Britain.

These three species are capable of interbreeding and this adds to the difficulty of identification.

Rosebay Willowherb and Great Willowherb are the other two species which one might encounter in a woodland. They are easy to identify – *see pages 176-178.*

American Willowherb

Pale Willowherb

Broad-leaved Willowherb

ROSEBAY WILLOWHERB

Chamerion angustifolium

Rosebay Willowherb is sometimes known as Fireweed, because it will often spring up in an area where there has been a bonfire. For this reason, it is classified as a pioneer, an opportunist species. In my woodland there are several areas where there have been fires.

After the Corsican Pines were felled, there was a lot of brash left lying about, so we hired a man with a JCB to scrape it all up into big brash heaps and set them on fire. As it turned out only about half of the brash piles were ever set alight because a change in wind direction meant that the burning had to stop.

In the end I was quite pleased that they were left because the brash heaps have provided a good little micro-habitat. Wrens use them for shelter and nesting and I am sure that many invertebrates are also living in them. They are reducing in size quite quickly and as they rot down and plants are starting to grow up out of them, so in a few years they will have all but disappeared.

The brash heaps that *were* burnt soon became marked by

*Rosebay Willowherb
colonising an old bonfire site*

tall pink spikes of Willowherb, mostly Rosebay. As time passes they are declining, as the influence of the bonfire, which gave rise to higher levels of potash, also reduces and the young trees grow up and the shade increases.

Rosebay Willowherb is a perennial, and has creeping rhizomes in the soil. It has long thin leaves and grows up to 1.5m and has beautiful spikes of purple flowers. These normally come out in midsummer and bloom for a long time. They are much frequented by bees and other insects. After the flowers are over, long thin seed pods develop, and these eventually split to release vast quantities of tiny seeds, about 3-400 per capsule, so approximately 80,000 per plant. The seeds have silky hairs to aid wind dispersal.

After the Second World War when there were lots of bomb sites around, this plant spread rapidly to colonise what were often inner city areas. Its spread was assisted by railway lines which in those days still had steam trains running on them and were subject to frequent fire from the sparks generated from their coal furnaces. The fire sites were quickly colonised and the resulting seeds were soon blown along by the trains. During that period the plant became known as Bombweed.

Even in the early 1960s, when I lived in the East End of London, there were still quite a lot of bomb sites, and as a small boy I was a collector of butterflies and moths, and I used to frequent these areas in search of specimens. The Rosebay Willowherb flowers attracted some butterflies, but what I was really looking out for were the caterpillars of various moths, such as the Elephant Hawkmoth caterpillar, which feeds on the leaves.

There are four different Hawkmoths which use the leaves as a food plant: the Elephant Hawkmoth, the Small Elephant Hawkmoth, the Striped Hawkmoth and the Bedstraw Hawkmoth. It was a happy hunting ground for a country boy uprooted from a small Essex village to find himself living just round the corner from West Ham football ground.

I only recall having found the Elephant Hawkmoth caterpillar.

Elephant Hawkmoth

Rosebay Willowherb spike

Great Willowherb

GREAT WILLOWHERB

Epilobium hirsutum

Great Willowherb is known by quite a few other names. As a child I knew it as Plums-and-custard, probably a name from my mother, but she did get things a bit wrong sometimes.

The purple petals are indeed a plum colour and the stamens and stigma in the centre are the colour of light custard, not the bright yellow packet variety but real egg yolk home-made custard.

It can easily reach 2m in height and it is a strong sturdy plant. The flowers are less concentrated than those of Rosebay Willowherb but are nonetheless quite showy. It will grow on the edge of woodland and tolerates some shade. It also seems to prefer a damp soil.

I have some growing in my section of Ninewells Wood in a corner where there is a bit of a drainage ditch which sometimes has water in it during the winter and spring. The plant is hairy and the leaves feel soft, like felt.

Its most-used common name is Codlins-and-cream, but it is also known as Apple-pie and Cherry-pie.

The seeds are produced in long capsules, each one producing a profusion of light fluffy windborne seeds.

This species, along with other Willowherbs, is the food plant of various caterpillars.

Great Willowherb

NETTLE-LEAVED BELLFLOWER

Campanula trachelium

Nettle-leaved Bellflower, is an impressive plant, growing up to 100cm tall with large bluish-purple bell-shaped flowers topping it off. This is a plant that is sold by many wild flower and seed suppliers, because it is imposing and rivals many cultivated garden plants. The plant is native.

I have seen this plant growing in the wild woodland patch of Kew Gardens where there were several of the white flowered variant. In France I see Nettle-leaved Bellflower quite often.

According to the BSBI it is recorded in 555 hectads out of 2810, and found mostly in southern regions, although records do extend into Scotland.

It likes shady places and will grow in fairly dense woodland. It is a plant that likes the soil rich, dryish and neutral-to-alkaline.

Sometimes called 'Bats-in-the-belfrey' it is also known as throatwort as it was thought to be a cure for tonsilitis.

Nettle-leaved Bellflower: the white variety

Nettle-leaved Bellflower with blue-purple flowers

St JOHN'S WORT: PALE and IMPERFORATE

Hypericum montanum and *Hypericum maculatum*

Pale St John's Wort, *H. montanum,* and the Imperforate St John's Wort, *H. maculatum,* are both semi-woodland St John's Wort species.

They both grow to about 1m, flower from July to September, are shade-tolerant but favour open woodland rides, edges of paths and firebreaks. The flowers are paler, or more creamy-yellow than some of the other St. John's Worts.

Imperforate St John's Wort is perhaps the more shade-tolerant of the two. It favours slightly more acidic soils than Pale St John's Wort. Imperforate St John's Wort has some black dots and dashes on the petals and randomly across the sepals and on the edges of the leaves. Its sepals are more rounded.

Pale St John's Wort does not have any black dots on the petals, but it does have them on the edges of sepals and leaves. The sepals on Pale St John's Wort are pointed.

Black dots are characteristic of this group of flowers. On some plants the dots and stripes on flowers are known as honey guides and they are there to direct the bees and pollinating insects to the nectar. However in this species the dots are around the edge and do not lead to the nectary. They are often referred to as 'glandular dots' which would suggest that they produce some sort of secretion.

St John's Wort contain various chemicals which can affect livestock adversely if eaten. Hypericin, in the oil glands of St John's Wort leaves and flowers, is the cause of this toxicity, but the effects are activated when bright sunlight causes the poison to circulate in the bloodstream. Different animals have differing tolerance to it. The minimum toxic dose of foliage for sheep is about four per cent of live weight. Horses are more sensitive to hypericin than cattle and sheep, with goats the least sensitive. Affected animals generally recover after 3-6 weeks once removed from access to the plant, but sheep with early signs of poisoning typically recover within twelve hours if they are moved indoors. Poisoning can reduce milk yield,

Pale St John's Wort

and cause abortions. The plant is more toxic when in flower and may contain more than fifty times more hypericin in early summer than in late winter. Narrow-leaved forms of the plant can be twice as toxic as broad-leaved biotypes. Plants become markedly more poisonous when the flowering shoots have grown 5-10cm high. Hay containing St John's Wort also causes poisoning so this plant is not therefore welcome in a grazing meadow but causes less harm in a wood.

Also in woodland you can find Trailing St John's Wort *Hypericum humifusum*. This is very small and quite difficult to spot. It only gets a few centimetres up off the gound and has little yellow flowers with the characteristic black dots on the edges of leaves, sepals and petals.

Imperforate St John's Wort

Peach-leaved Bellflower

BELLFLOWERS: GIANT and PEACH-LEAVED

Campanula latifolia and Campanula persicifolia

There are several species of Bellflower in Britain and they are all, with one exception, in the genus *Campanula*. The one that is familiar to most people is the Harebell but this is a grassland species, not found in woodland. In terms of woodland species there is Nettle-leaved Bellflower, Ivy-leaved Bellflower and Spreading Bellflower which are all dealt with separately on other pages. The two similar species which I have put together are Giant and Peach leaved Bellflower. The two photographs are of the Peach-leaved Bellflower.

These Bellflowers were very conspicuous and growing beside the road in a wooded area. They were identifiable as the Peach-leaved species because the splits in the petals did not cut back deeply and each stem had only a few flowers on it. Many of the flowers had attracted little metallic green beetles, no doubt helping out with the pollination process. The stigma which splits into three, typical of the genus, is very noticeable.

They are not native but are found in Britain, mainly in the south and frequently they are garden escapes. They are perennials so once established they will survive for many years if undisturbed.

The Giant Bellflower is a native species of our woodlands. It has deeper splits between the five fused petals that make up the bell. The flower spike has more flowers than the Peach-leaved species and it has a lot of leaves along the whole length of the stalk.

There is a public house in Selby Yorkshire called the Giant Bellflower, an unusual name for a pub, so named because a famous herbalist, Thomas Johnson, was born in Selby early in the seventeenth century. He recorded numerous examples of the Giant Bellflower on the banks of the River Ouse flowing through Selby. He published many books about his botanical excursions and was mortally wounded in the Civil War when fighting for the Royalists.

Peach-leaved Bellflower

ORPINE

Hylotelephium telephium

Orpine in a hedgerow

This plant has a host of common names such as Livelong, Frog's-stomach, Harping Johnny, Life-everlasting, Live-forever, Midsummer-men, Orphan John and Witch's Moneybags. The references to long life arise because it is a succulent plant and pieces that get broken off survive a long time before they dry up and wither away.

Orpine is a distinctive flower, related to the white-flowered Stonecrops, to which it bears a clear resemblance, but it is much bigger, growing to about 100cm and it has pink flowers.

It is a perennial herb, found on woodland borders, hedge banks, roadsides, rocky banks and in limestone pavements, often in very small but persistent colonies. It is sometimes found in ancient woodlands, but frequently fails to flower in this habitat. Unfortunately this is another plant which has suffered from garden cultivated individuals interbreeding with the wild stock so that now we have a complete muddle of escapees, native and hybrid plants.

Orpine flower head

IVY-LEAVED BELLFLOWER

Whalenbergia hederacea

This is the one species of Bellflower growing in Britain which is *not* in the genus *Campanula*.

It is quite a rare species, found mainly in Wales and south-west England with small numbers found along the south coast and in a few isolated areas in the north of England and southern Ireland. Fellow botanist Jonathan Hickling kindly directed me to some growing near Dunsop Bridge in the Forest of Bowland, Lancashire. Only 195miles from where I live! Not knowing of any closer to hand, I made the journey.

According to the BSBI it is found in 314 hectads in Britain, mostly in Wales. It grows in damp, wet or boggy places on acidic soils, including open woodlands. It flowers in July and August. The ones in Lancashire, however, flower a little later and I saw them there in mid-September.

The flowers are very small, about 5mm across, and are light blue with slightly darker veins running down each of the five petals

Ivy-leaved Bellflower

that fuse together to make the bell. They have a typical bellflower and the stigma which splits into three. They are held singly on long delicate stalks. The leaves bear a resemblance to Ivy but they are less angular.

Recently I found them only four miles from home! It was on the side of a shady and damp path in the Forest of Dean, albeit a very small patch.

Ivy-leaved Bellflower in The Forest of Bowland

SELF-HEAL

Prunella vulgaris

Self-heal is a little wild flower which is prolific, but easily overlooked. It prefers alkaline or neutral soils and is shade tolerant so can be found in open woodland. Close up, it is a pretty little plant.

It is low growing and spreads out in a mat of stems and leaves. When it flowers, the stem does a right angle turn and grows upright for a few centimetres to elevate the flower. This species is another in the group known as Labiates. Its square stem is covered with small hairs and the usual lipped flower is an attractive purple blue. It flowers from June onward and keeps flowering right through to November.

At each junction along the stem (node) the plant is able to produce roots and thereby can root itself from the heel of the plant. The upper lip of Self-heal is in the shape of a hook, and billhooks and sickles were the main causes of wounds in Medieval farming communities. Therefore, it was once believed that this plant would be useful in curing such injuries. Other common names for it are Hook-heal and Sickle-wort, supporting the idea that its name comes from medicinal uses. Self-heal was also made into a syrup as a cure for internal injuries. Scholars had already identified the plant as the herb used by Dioscorides, the Greek physician, to cure inflammation of the throat and tonsils. The Latin name *Prunella* comes from the Germanic word for sore throat. It has also been used to stop bleeding and as an antiseptic.

Clearly a plant that has been used in the past for various curative processes.

Self-heal

COMMON VALERIAN

Valeriana officinalis

Common Valerian flowerheads

Valerian has long been ascribed various healing properties and contains a number of compounds which affect metabolism. Products extracted from the plant are commercially available, especially an oily extract from the root which may have some calming sedative effects, but there is no connection between Valerian and valium.

Common Valerian is one of four species of Valerian found in Britain. The others are Red Valerian, Marsh Valerian, and Pyrenean Valerian.

Common Valerian is a perennial and it is found throughout Britain in woodlands and in some grasslands. It flowers between June and August and the flowers are white, sometimes with a hint of pink. The buds are often pink. The individual flowers are grouped into a small domed umbel. Usually the plant has three groups of flowers at the top of the stalk: one larger cluster right at the top and two subsidiary clusters which angle out a little lower down.

The individual flowers comprise five petals which fuse together lower down to make a short tube. Very occasionally a flower will be made up of just four petals. They have a slight smell of vanilla. The leaves are compound, made up of several leaflets. They are jagged and arranged in pairs along the stem.

Valerian has an unusual distribution in Britain, seeming to avoid the central spine of England. They are found in East Anglia, throughout Scotland and Wales, along the Welsh borders and in the south-west of Britain.

Common Valerian leaves with bramble above

BURDOCK

Arctium species

Burdock does what its name implies. It has a seed head which is a burr covered with hooks and big, dock-shaped leaves. The leaves of Burdock are soft and hairy – not shiny and hairless like true dock although the shape is similar.

There are several species of Burdock and there are also hybrids. They are all in the genus *Arctium*. From the most robust to the most frail, there is Greater Burdock, Intermediate Burdock, Lesser Burdock and Wood Burdock.

Greater Burdock *Arctium lappa* is the larger plant and can be distinguished because the flowering area (the purple bit) is flat and does not dome up as it does in Lesser Burdock, *Arctium minus*.

The other three burdocks are all biennials and all have the purple burr flowers which flower from midsummer onwards. They grow in a variety of places including woodland edges and rides.

The difference between Greater and Lesser Burdock is the size and the fact that the leaf stems (petioles) are solid in Greater Burdock and hollow in Lesser Burdock. The flower

Burdock seed heads

Lesser Burdock

stalks are shorter in Lesser Burdock, less than 2cm, whilst in the case of Greater Burdock they are 2.5cm or more.

Wood burdock *Arctium nemorosum* resembles a tall growing Lesser Burdock and is most likely to be encountered in a woodland. The flower heads (capitula) are arranged in the same fashion in loose flower-clusters growing in the form of a raceme. Wood Burdock's branches curve downwards rather than spreading rigidly like Lesser Burdock. Wood Burdock flowers are larger and egg-shaped. The individual florets that make up each composite flower of Wood Burdock are roughly the same length as the surrounding bracts, while on Lesser Burdock they are longer.

Dandelion and Burdock is a drink which most people over the age of sixty will remember, although it is apparently enjoying a renaissance. I recall the lorry delivering various flavoured fizzy drinks to the door when I was a child. We returned our empty bottles as there was a deposit on them and selected the flavours we wanted for the next week. Cream

Soda, Cherryade, Lemonade and of course Dandelion and Burdock were the favourites.

The fizzy drink in the 1960s probably did not contain any Dandelion or Burdock, just chemicals. The flavour of burdock was similar to that of a volatile oil found in a plant called Sassafras (used in America to make Sarsaparilla) and this replaced the burdock root in the 1960s.

Thankfully, there are now some producers making Dandelion and Burdock which once again contains the proper ingredients. Historically, the drink was a brew from the stewed roots of the burdock and dandelion mixed with a little honey and then fermented. This resulted in a mildly alcoholic brew with a bit of fizz, similar to natural Ginger beer.

Burdock roots are now grown commercially, especially in Japan, where it is known as gobō. It is the Greater Burdock *Arctium lappa* which is grown commercially for its culinary and medicinal uses, and of course Dandelion and Burdock fizzy pop!

Greater Burdock

ENCHANTER'S NIGHTSHADE

Circaea lutetiana

Enchanter's Nightshade is a woodland plant which reaches its peak of flowering in late summer. This is very much a woodland species. Some of the plants I have included in this book are plants which tolerate shade and so grow in a woodland but also in hedgerows and other habitats. This one is exclusively a woodland wild flower.

It is very delicate plant with little starry flowers that need to be looked at closely in order to see their structure. They have what looks like four white petals, two up and two down. However there are actually only two petals which are strongly divided into two lobes and so they appear as four. It is most unusual for a flower to have just two petals. Indeed

Enchanter's Nightshade

I cannot think of another that has this few. Protruding from the centre of these flowers are two stamens, flanking a single stigma which splits at the end, resembling a snake's tongue.

The leaves look similar to those of Dog's Mercury: perhaps not so long nor so dark green but they are easy to muddle up because they grow in similar habitats.

The name Enchanter's Nightshade comes from its scientific name *Circaea lutetiana*. Circe was an enchantress who seduced Ulysses, in Homer's *Odyssey*. She used a potion which may have contained Enchanters Nightshade along with other plants to turn Odysseus' shipmates into pigs.

There is another connection between this plant and Homer, but this time it is from *The Iliad*, and this time it relates to alternative common names for it which are Sorcerer of Paris and Paris Nightshade which alludes to Paris of Troy.

Enchanter's Nightshade is listed as an ingredient in many ancient herbal and magical compendiums, but there is often reference to its berries. Since this plant has sticky burrs, but no berries, one can only assume that these texts are referring to a different plant. Likely candidates include Bittersweet or Woody Nightshade *Solanum dulcamara*, which is native to Europe and Asia; or evenmore likely, Deadly Nightshade, also known as Belladonna, *Atropa belladonna,* which has a long history of use in medicine, magic and cosmetics.

Enchanter's Nightshade flower spike

Hemp Agrimony

AUTUMN

(SEPTEMBER, OCTOBER and NOVEMBER)

There are not many shade-tolerant woodland plants that flower in the latter months of the year. A few come into flower in September but whilst you will still get flowers in bloom during October and November, none actually start to flower in those months.

Of the true woodland species, it is only Sowbread (also called Wild Cyclamen) and Meadow Saffron (Autumn Crocus) that are found in the heart of the woods. There are others, such as Water Pepper, found on the edges of woods or, as in the case of Heather, in open heath woodlands.

However, by the beginning of November, the first hints of the next year may already be making their appearance. Depending on the weather, one or two Primroses may start to flower. As the hazel bushes lose their golden leaves, next year's male catkins are already there. They are small and green but very visible and some may elongate and turn yellow with pollen even before the end of the year.

In the same way as the first flowers of the year are important for overwintering insects, especially bees, so too are these final flowers of the yearly cycle, especially Hemp Agrimony, Ploughman's Spikenard, Heather and Goldenrod. If one walks past a woodland wall covered with Ivy, its flowers will now be alive with insects and one can hear it buzzing.

HEMP AGRIMONY

Eupatorium cannabinum

Hemp Agrimony is a tall dominant flower found in damp shady woodlands and boggy woodland carr habitats. It can grow up to 2m tall and has pink flowers which form a sort of platform rather like an umbelliferous flower. It flowers in August and September.

The name Hemp derives from the fact that its leaves bear some resemblance to those of the cannabis plant which is also called hemp – no connection.

There is quite a lot of Hemp Agrimony in my wood. It often grows on the edge of forest rides and presumably the flowers produce plenty of nectar as they attract a lot of insects, particularly butterflies. I have seen Comma, Small Tortoiseshell, and Fritillaries visiting the flowers.

The photograph below shows a Brown Hairstreak, a particularly rare butterfly, on Hemp Agrimony.

The plant is in the Daisy family, and is most closely related to the Aster. Each individual flower is like a little Daisy with long thin petals.

Hemp Agrimony has been used as a herbal remedy for centuries. The genus name *Eupatorium* can be traced back to the Ancient Greek king Mithridates Eupator (120-63 BC), who was the first to use species in this genus to combat all sorts of ailments, and it probably does have some laxative powers, should such be needed.

With Brown Hairstreak butterfly

Hemp Agrimony

PLOUGHMAN'S SPIKENARD

Inula conyzae

Ploughman's Spikenard particularly favours steep, chalky woodland slopes surrounded by Ash trees.

Recently, walking with a friend who is a keen naturalist, we came across some Ploughman's Spikenard. He explained that nard is a perfumed oil used in many different religious ceremonies, not just Christian. Nard was extracted from the roots of an Indian plant called Spikenard, and in the Bible Mary, sister of Lazarus, uses a jar of pure nard to anoint the feet of Jesus. My friend would know about this as he is a retired bishop. Ploughman's Spikenard is not the same plant as that used in biblical times but its roots do also have a fragrance, hence the 'nard'. It is claimed that Ploughmen and other country folk used to hang up Ploughman's spikes in their houses to make the air smell nice.

It favours alkaline soils and is tolerant of some shade. It has composite flowers which are yellow with outer surrounding bracts which are pink to purple. The flowers are small and arranged in a loose umbel. The flower stem which is also purple and covered with fine hairs can achieve a height of over 1m. It flowers in August and September.

It is a member of the Daisy family and is a biennial. By the end of its first year it will have produced a rosette of leaves which look very similar to those of a foxglove at the same stage.

Ploughman's Spikenard flower

Ploughman's Spikenard

NARROW-LIPPED and GREEN HELLEBORINE

Epipactis leptochila and E. phyllanthes

These two Helleborines are in the *Epipactis* genus and are both rare. They have more chunky flowers than most British orchids (perhaps with the exception of Insect Orchids). They are not unlike the exotic orchids sold in garden centres, only they are much smaller and not so brightly coloured.

I have grouped the Narrow-lipped and Green Helleborine together because they look fairly similar and they both flower in August, unlike the Narrow-leaved and White Helleborine which bloom early in May or June. The latter two are in a different genus, *Cephalanthera*.

The Narrow-lipped and Green Helleborines favour woodlands with alkaline soils with an underlying limestone or chalk bedrock.

I found a single orchid growing in some woodland close to the River Wye. I knew it was a Helleborine and suspected that it was not the common Broad-leaved species as its leaves were not very wide. I took some photographs of it whilst in bud but then I had the misfortune of having to go on holiday! When I came back a couple of weeks later I immediately went to see

Narrow-lipped Helleborine detail

how it was getting on and it was gone, probably eaten by deer or rabbits. The woods where it was growing support several species of deer.

I have revisited these woods on several occasions, not least because they are said to also support the White Helleborine, although I have not yet found it growing there.

Then, one August I found it, growing exactly where I had seen the specimen some years earlier. On close inspection I was able to confirm that it was the Narrow-lipped Helleborine, which was a first for me.

The Green Helleborine is found predominantly in Dorset, Kent, Norfolk and Cumberland and in a few places in Wales. It is absent from Scotland. It favours Beech woods. Its distinguishing characteristic is the large bright green, swollen and ridged receptacle located behind the petals. It flowers from July to mid-August.

Narrow-lipped Helleborine

Green Helleborine

WILD ANGELICA

Angelica sylvestris

I see a lot of Wild Angelica growing in Ninewells Wood. It likes damp soils and will tolerate some shade. There is a wide forestry path running through the centre of the wood which is quite wet on both sides and often there are puddles which are semi-permanent. This is where a lot of the Wild Angelica grows. Hemp Agrimony, various thistles and Knapweed also grow along this path and these attract a lot of butterflies, including the Silver Washed Fritillary which is an absolute stunner.

Wild Angelica is in the carrot family, an umbellifer along with Cow Parsley, Hogweed and others. It grows to 2.5m and the flowers are often pink. The stalk is pink or purple.

The other umbellifer which has this characteristic is the deadly Hemlock, but Hemlock has a more blotchy purple colouration. Wild Angelica flowers from July to September, later in the year than many other umbellifers.

What is unusual about this plant is that the flowers attract a lot of flies, hoverflies and wasps – but not butterflies.

Angelica was used as a vegetable in the past. I would recommend caution as it could be mistaken for Hemlock, although the latter has a really disgusting smell.

Wild Angelica showing purple stalks

Trailing Tormentil

TRAILING TORMENTIL
Potentilla anglica

Trifoliate leaves

Trailing Tormentil is one of the Potentilla group of wild flowers which includes Silverweed, the Cinquefoils and Barren Strawberry.

Cinquefoil and Tormentil are most similar to Trailing Tormentil. Cinquefoil has small yellow flowers, usually with five petals whilst Tormentil's yellow flowers usually have four but occasionally five. Cinquefoil has leaves with five leaflets, hence *cinq feuille*, whereas Tormentil has three.

Trailing Tormentil is a plant that can grow in lightly shaded woodland habitats, although it does not like deep shade so it is generally found on the edges of woodlands. It prefers acidic soils.

Trailing Tormentil has petioles and its flowers are 14–18mm across.

There are several hybrids and this can cause confusion.

NIPPLEWORT

Lapsana communis

Nipplewort

This is an annual plant which grows in shady places on the edges of woods and in hedgerows, and as a garden weed. It can grow as high as 80cm and has an open branched structure with lots of little yellow flowers. In my garden it only grows up to about 30cm and produces only 10-20 flowers because it is often competing with taller garden plants which shade it.

It could be confused with Wall Lettuce but the leaves are different. The plant normally has about ten ray florets arranged in two concentric circles. The outer ring has slightly longer petals and the inner ring slightly shorter. In the centre are just a few disc florets, about ten, and the number of disc florets is always the same as the number of ray florets.

It is perhaps not the most inspirational flower but at least it has a memorable name.

GOLDENROD

Solidago virgaurea

There are not many woodland plants which flower late in the year and even then they are mostly those which are woodland margin plants not found in the depths of a wood. The European Goldenrod is such a plant.

The wild species is very different to the giant specimens which are part of the traditional English garden. In gardens, Goldenrod grows to about 1.5m tall, often alongside Michaelmas Daisies which are generally a bit shorter than the Goldenrods but both flower at roughly the same time, late summer to early autumn.

Goldenrod are members of the Aster family and produce typical compositae or daisy-type flowers with a circle of ray florets, commonly referred to as the petals. These surround a central group of disc florets. Both the ray and disc florets are yellow. The ray florets are not particularly well developed so at a casual glance the flowers just look like little yellow 'bobbles' and can be confused with Ragwort, the flowers of which are similar but the leaves are quite different.

Goldenrod spike

LING

Calluna vulgaris

Bell Heather (*Erica cinerea*)

There are lots of species of Heather, most of which have the scientific name *Erica*. However the most common in Britain's woodlands is *Calluna vulgaris*, often called Ling. The flower of Ling is made up of four petals and four sepals whereas in the *Erica* genus, the flower is made up of five of each.

There was a very small amount of Ling growing in my wood when I bought it some years ago. At that time, my wood was a Corsican Pine forest and very dark, so the heather was up against it. Once the Pines were felled and the disturbance from heavy forestry machinery was becoming a fading memory, heather started to spring up everywhere. The seeds can survive in the soil for 70 years or more. The first plants flowered within a year of the felling and within two years many areas were pink with a carpet of heather in flower in August and September.

Individually the Ling flowers are small and lilac pink; not as impressive as the Erica species. There is a little Bell Heather *Erica cinerea* also growing in my wood which has larger flowers which are decidedly purple. These are not really a woodland species, preferring dry heathland, whereas Ling will grow in many woods, especially if they are fairly open. The Bell Heather flowers a few weeks earlier than Ling. Very occasionally Ling has white flowers and this is the so-called 'lucky heather' that many years ago gypsies would try to sell.

Ling is the main food plant of grouse. They eat the young tips of the plant but as it ages it becomes rather scrubby. It is, after all, a woody plant and is really a very low-growing bush, so after about ten years of growth it is largely woody with very short green growing tips and therefore not so appetising for grouse. However in this state it still provides a good sheltered place for the grouse to hide and nest, so in order to maintain a good population of grouse, both young heather for food and old heather for shelter is required. On large estates in Scotland where grouse shooting takes place, regular controlled burning of the moorland has traditionally been undertaken. After burning, seeds in the soil quickly germinate and after a couple of years a lawn of young heather develops providing good food for the grouse. Ten years on this becomes scrubby and old and needs burning again and so it continues.

Amazingly for such a small, plump bird, Red grouse can reach speeds of eighty miles per hour soon after they have taken off, making them difficult to shoot.

Other species associated with heather are the Emperor Moth, lizards, adders, and bees. Heather honey is a speciality in some areas.

Ling (Calluna vulgaris)

SOWBREAD

Cyclamen hederifolium

Sowbread

Sowbread is a Wild Cyclamen. It flowers in the late summer and autumn and has pink or occasionally white flowers. The derivation of the name is supposedly that pigs and wild boar uproot the tubers and eat them, so it is bread (food) for sows. I prefer the name Wild Cyclamen. It is highly toxic to humans and some other animals, so I am not sure that pigs do actually eat the tubers.

Wild Cyclamen, *C. hederifolium,* was introduced into Britain in Tudor times, and seems to be increasingly frequent in woodlands and hedgerows, particularly near to a relic of habitation or former cultivation. It was first recorded in the wild as early as 1597. Originally it came from southern Europe and Turkey.

The leaves grow up from the tuber in the autumn and are then present through the winter, dying in spring. The plant then goes dormant through the summer until in the early autumn when it flowers. Unusually, the roots do not grow out of the underside of the corm. They grow from the top and then bend over and grow down into the soil.

Another interesting feature of this plant is that when the seeds are produced, the stalk on which the seed pod is attached bends downwards and grows in a spiral, thus corkscrewing the seed into the ground. Ants sometimes collect the seeds and take them some distance from the plant, so aiding their distribution. This use of ants is called *myrmecochory*. Several woodland plants rely on ants to help their dispersal. Some plants actually have a little lump on the seed called an elaiosome which is food for the ants. In the case of this cyclamen, the seeds are covered with a sticky substance which the ants like and this is why they carry them off.

WATER-PEPPER

Persicaria hydropiper

There are three Water-peppers: Water-pepper *Persicaria hydropiper*, Tasteless Water-pepper *Persicaria mitis* and Least Water-pepper *Percicaria minor*. Other species in the genus include the Bistorts, Redleg and Pale Persicaria.

Water-pepper has white or pink flowers. The other two species have pink to slightly red flowers. The flowers form a drooping spike and can be found from June to the end of September. I normally find Water-pepper growing along wet muddy woodland footpaths.

It is not the sort of plant that makes one instantly stop to admire, being low growing and straggly.

Water-pepper

MEADOW SAFFRON

Colchicum autumnale

Meadow Saffron

Meadow Saffron is sometime known as Autumn Crocus although it is not actually a member of the Crocus family. It is one of the few woodland flowers which comes into bloom in the autumn.

Meadow Saffron flowers are more delicate than most of the spring-flowering crocuses and are always purple. The difference between Meadow Saffron and crocuses, to which it is unrelated, is that the flowers of Meadow Saffron have a white stigma, which is just visible in the photograph. True crocuses have a yellow stigma which is saffron. Meadow Saffron has six stamens and the crocuses only have three.

The flowers emerge after the leaves have died back and this gives rise to Meadow Saffron's other name of Naked Ladies.

This plant contains a substance called *colchicum* which is poisonous, and has resulted in fatalities when people have collected the leaves, mistaking them for those of wild garlic. Throughout the ages, extracts of colchicum have been used as a way of warding off gout, and it is now possible to buy preparations of colchicine to prevent its recurrence.

Colchicum is also an important source of chemical in the plant breeding field which can induce plants to double their chromosome number. This is important because, if a hybrid between two related plants is artificially produced then it will normally be sterile because the chromosomes from one parent will not match up with those of the other parent. The only way to propagate a new hybrid plant used to be via cuttings or via tubers or bulbs: slow and not always easy. Then along comes colchicine which can double the chromosome number so that they can now be matched up and a new fertile hybrid is produced.

This treatment has been used on many species including Cannabis, Gingers and Zinnias.

As with so many wild plants, Meadow Saffron has declined in recent years. This is partly because landowners who farm sheep and cattle have removed it because it is poisonous to livestock. The heartland for the species is the Cotswolds, the borders of the Wye Valley and in some of the Welsh hills. Garden escapes are possible anywhere in the country.

Snowdrops on wooded banks of the River Wye

WINTER

(DECEMBER, JANUARY and FEBRUARY)

It is such a joy to see the first flowers of the year. Those brave early flowers in the depths of winter are forerunners of spring and on a sunny day in January, the Lesser Celandine or Winter Aconite really do gladden one's heart. Several of these early flowering plants are a real lifeline for the bees which have over-wintered and by now might be in desperate need of a calorific top-up. A plant which is particularly useful in this respect is the Winter Heliotrope which advertises its presence by its strong vanilla scent. It can begin flowering even before the final Christmas presents have been purchased. However, it is an introduced species and very much a mixed blessing as it spreads rapidly, and its large leaves can soon out-compete most other woodland species.

Especially these days with our changing climate, all sorts wild flowers can be found flowering in the early months of the year. What was an odd occurrence now becomes increasingly the norm. Do not be surprised to see some of the early spring flowers making a premature appearance in winter, flowers such as the Primrose, Green Alkanet and Barren Strawberry, all of which can often flower at this time. There are also several woodland flowers that have a preferred flowering period or a peak flowering time, but which can be present at almost any time of the year. I am thinking of White Dead Nettle, Herb Robert and Gorse. The concept of the New Year's Day birdwatch is familiar to many, in which those who like to get out in the fresh air after the excesses of Christmas count the species they spot that day. Not so well known is the tradition for some who go out for a walk on New Year's Day to see how many wild flowers they can find in bloom.

Why not try it?

WINTER HELIOTROPE

Petasites fragrans

At first sight Winter Heliotrope could be mistaken for a rather scruffy bit of Butterbur, but a more detailed investigation would reveal that it is a different species. It has a powerful vanilla scent and it is closely related to Butterbur. They are both in the genus *Petasites*. The leaves of Winter Heliotrope are rounded, soft, downy and large. The pinky-white flowers show in deepest winter, and the plant is shade tolerant. The genus name comes from the Greek word *petasos*, which are felt hats worn by shepherds.

The Winter Heliotrope hails from North Africa but now inhabits much of Europe. It is invasive, competitive and tends to obliterate all other wild flowers in the area.

Winter Heliotrope was first brought to Britain in 1806 for use as a garden plant. It flowers in December through to January or February so it adds interest during the winter months. By 1835 it had established itself in the wild and is now a regular woodland sight across Britain. Its poor tolerance of low temperatures has prevented its spread into northern Britain, although it might well start to appear further north as temperatures increase with climate change. Only male plants are found in Britain so it can only spread asexually, by gradually growing via its roots through an area, or by a piece of the plant being uprooted and transported to a new location, most likely by man but just possibly by large wild animals such as boar or deer.

Winter Heliotrope is a good source of nectar and thus beneficial to bees in the early spring. It is not very tolerant of frost, as one might expect, given that it originates from warmer parts of the world but it quickly recovers after a knock back.

Helios was the personification of the sun in Greek mythology. He was the son of the Titan Hyperion and his wife the Titaness Theia. The word *trope* in this context means movement. Phototropism describes the process whereby plants grow towards the light. Geotropism is positive in roots which grow towards the pull of gravity, and negative in shoots which grow away from the pull of gravity. Heliotrope is so named because of its movement towards the sun. Heliotrope flowers, like sunflowers, follow the sun through the day.

Winter Heliotrope

Snowdrops: one of more than 500 cultivars

SNOWDROPS

Galanthus nivalis

Snowdrops

Snowdrops are described as 'naturalised' meaning that they are not native British plants but have become part of the British countryside, growing alongside other wild flowers without any help or input from man.

There are many different species of Snowdrop. The one we have in Britain is called *Galanthus nivalis*. The name was created by Linnaeus – *gala* means milk, *anthos* means flower and *nivalis* refers to snow, so it is a milk-coloured flower which blooms when there is snow. Sounds sensible to me.

Most species of Snowdrop come from the Middle East. *Galanthus nivalis* is the most widespread, being found not only in the Middle East but right across Europe into France, Belgium and Holland. There are also many garden cultivars. Man cannot resist trying to improve upon nature, so we now have double Snowdrops and strains in which the green colour on the petals is missing or has been substituted with yellow. Man has produced over 500 different Snowdrop cultivars and one has to wonder why!

The Snowdrop's petals are strictly tepals as the flowers do not have separate sepals and petals, but an all-in-one version which does the job of sepals (protecting the flower whilst in bud) and petals (looking pretty and attracting insects).

It has three outer tepals, the longer white concave ones and three inner tepals which are shorter, form a little tube and have green markings.

Snowdrops are often the first woodland flowers to bloom in spring although Aconites also flower at about the same time. Snowdrops might have been introduced into Britain by the Romans, but it is more likely that they were introduced in the 16th century. They spread widely by increasing the number of bulbs in the ground and not by seeds. This is quite a slow process but one that does result in dense colonies forming.

LAUREL-SPURGE

Daphne laureola

It is debatable whether this plant should be included in a book on woodland wild flowers, as it is essentially a little shrub, but then again the same could be said of Gorse and strictly speaking even Heather and Bilberry, yet these have been included. There is no hard and fast rule as to where a herb (in the sense of a type of plant) stops and a shrub begins. One distinction is said to be that shrubs have several woody stems emanating from one point and herbs have a single stem.

However, when Laurel-spurge is young it will have just one stem, and many herbs, such as Dahlias and Pelargoniums, have several stems, so take your pick. Thyme, which I think of as a herb both in the botanical and the culinary sense, is classified as a sub-shrub!

Sometimes also referred to as Spurge-laurel it is neither a Spurge nor a Laurel. Its leaves do look like Laurel in that they are leathery, shiny and the same shape as those of the Laurel,

Leathery leaves of Laurel-spurge

Laurel-spurge flowers

but it is not a Laurel. The flowers do not look like those of Spurge and in fact its only resemblance to Spurge is the overall shape of the plant. The flowers are produced early in the year and are somewhat obscured by the spreading and imposing leaves. They are small and tubular and are a light green. Some say they produce a strong scent but I have never detected any from the ones I have come across. These flowers are insect-pollinated so a strong smell would be an advantage. I suspect that their pollination is not very efficient as I cannot recall ever seeing large numbers of fruits, certainly not as many fruits as flowers. If every apple blossom produced an apple then the trees would be overwhelmed. Spurge-Laurel is a very poisonous plant. The black clusters of fruits are eaten by birds but that does not mean that we can!

Laurel-spurge favours heavy alkaline soils, particularly in Beech woods. For some reason it is more rare in Wales particularly as you go further west. It is classified as native but quite often its presence is due to garden escapes. It is also often found in woods that owe their existence to pheasant shooting. Gamekeepers like to encourage a good dense layer of low-growing shrubs and Snowberry is one favoured plant, as is Laurel-spurge, as it provides good cover for the game.

A young plant

BUTCHER'S BROOM

Ruscus aculeatus

My first encounter with Butcher's Broom was when I was 17 and studying A-level Biology. It was a specimen preserved in alcohol, a faded army green and it smelled alcoholic. The reason for studying it was that this plant has a peculiar adaptation to reduce water loss. Its leaves are tiny, almost invisible, so to compensate for this reduction in photosynthetic surface, the stem has developed large, flattened protuberances which look exactly like leaves and are green. In the photograph the oval green spikes that look like leaves are actually flattened extensions of the stem, technically called *cladodes*. The group of indoor plants known as Christmas Cactus, are typical of this.

There are a couple of things that are puzzling about this adaptation. The first is why a woodland plant should need to develop an adaptation to prevent water loss? Woodlands are blessed with humid, shady, cool conditions and they have a soil that has a good layer of humus and leaf litter which is damp and retains water. Secondly, one of the important features of

Butcher's Broom, the female flower

leaves are the stomata, little pores on the underside which allow carbon dioxide to enter the leaf to be used for photosynthesis. Presumably the flattened stems will not have this advantage and so the efficiency of the photosynthetic process will be reduced, which is not a good thing in a shady woodland.

After flowering very early in the year, Butcher's Broom produces large round seed pods which are initially green but ripen to a rich red. Most bushes produce only a few berries, normally in ones and twos, which are possibly eaten by birds or small mammals.

Recently I found this plant growing in a small woodland reserve on the outskirts of Gloucester. Butcher's Broom has a southerly distribution in Britain and I suspect that this is on the northern edge of its range. There were only about eight bushes growing in one small area. It is almost certain that they were planted, as the reserve is a remnant of a former garden which surrounded a large house, now long gone. I could not find any young plants, so it is not spreading. Butcher's Broom is dioecious, so has male flowers on one plant and female on another. I only found plants with female flowers at this site. The first flush of flowers are very early and continue for a couple of months before swelling into little round fruits. These eventually develop into the large round red fruits, about the size of a large pea.

The low bushes are around 75cm tall. The flowers are small and develop in the centre of the phylloclade. They have three petals and three sepals and are green with a slight purple blush edging. This structure is reminiscent of Snowdrops, to which this plant is indeed related, both being part of the *Asparagaceae*.

Being a former garden, the reserve had several other woodland wild flowers showing through: lots of Winter Aconites in flower, a few Snowdrops, and leaves of Cyclamen, Lesser Periwinkle, and probably Bluebells and Daffodils. It is certainly an asset for that area of Gloucester.

Butcher's Broom berries

Growing in a Gloucestershire wood

WINTER ACONITE

Eranthis hyemalis

Winter Aconite flower and bracts

Winter Aconites are one of the first plants to flower in the year, often contending with snow and frost.

The plant reproduces in two ways. It has tuberous roots which enable it to overwinter and to spread gradually. The flowers also produce seeds which can lead to a more rapid spread. The yellow flowers are held above a circle of green bracts that could be confused for sepals. Next come a ring of six yellow sepals, which one might assume were the petals. There are a large number of yellow stamens, but only six carpels which are the female parts.

It is not a native British plant; it is native to France, Italy and the Balkans. It has become naturalised in some areas of Britain and has been growing in the wild here since the 1830s. It is widely planted in gardens and parks, but it also now forms extensive wild patches in woods throughout Britain, but mostly in the south Midlands, the south-east and the east.

It is a member of the Buttercup family and is most closely related to Monkshood. Both contain a similar poison to that present in the secretions from toad's skin.

Winter Aconite contains several cardiac glycosides, ingestion of substantial quantities of which leads to nausea, vomiting, diarrhoea, colic, bradycardia, disturbed vision, dyspnoea and finally cardiac arrest.

Best not to snack on it then!

GIANT BUTTERBUR

Petasites japonicus

Giant Butterbur is an introduced (alien) species. It prefers wet and shady places and is often found in boggy woodlands and carr habitats.

It flowers before the leaves are fully formed and the flowers look a cross between a triffid and a cauliflower. They are white, bulky and look alien. When the leaves emerge later in the year, they are very large and swamp smaller woodland plants.

It has another interesting name – Fuki Bog Rhubarb! It originates from Japan and is so named because, after it has flowered, it produces enormous rhubarb-like leaves. It has now been introduced into many parts of the world, and is edible, consumed particularly in some Japanese cuisine. **Proper preparation in order to remove its toxins is essential.**

Late snow and frosts can cause damage to this early-flowering plant. It is sensitive to low temperatures, and the central flowers in each flower head can be affected, turning brown and failing to develop.

Giant Butterbur showing slight frost damage

Large group of Giant Butterburs

Stinking Hellebore

STINKING HELLEBORE
Helleborus foetidus

They flower in January and for most of the year might be overlooked as low bushy perennial plants in a woodland. I came across a huge colony on some oak-treed hills literally a few hundred yards from where I live, when I stumbled across several patches where they were the dominant plant. I would estimate that there were between 150-250 individual plants growing in an area.

The leaves are palmate and vary in colour from dark green to dark purple in winter. The new leaves start to develop early and even in January some of the plants bear tufts of new smaller leaves. The stems sometimes have purple blotches on them.

The flowers are a light green or yellow and sometimes the sepals, which look like petals, are edged with purple. The flower shoots have bracts which are the same colour as the sepals. The combination of flowers and bracts is bright, and attracts one's attention, especially at a time of year when few other plants have bright green foliage. Presumably the bees and other insect pollinators also find it easy to spot them in January.

After the flowers are over, large seed pods develop. They look a bit like pea pods but there are three fused together. The plants largely propagate by the dispersal of their seeds. Individual plants only live for four or five years, so they are short-lived perennials. Although they are called 'stinking' they only smell if you crush the leaves. Stinking Hellebore is, however, poisonous and in the past it was used to rid people of worms. The amount administered must have been critical as too much would kill not only the worms but also their host!

The population I found was growing in their proper habitat which is steep, limestone and somewhat craggy with scattered trees giving partial shade.

Lesser Celandine

LESSER CELANDINE

Ficaria verna

Lesser Celandine is probably the first native woodland plant to come into flower each year. There are some garden species such as Aconites and Snowdrops which may pip them to the post, but Lesser Celandine is native and a very early blooming woodland plant.

Any growing as weeds in the garden can flower right through the winter.

Lesser Celandine is in the Buttercup family, the *Ranunculaceae*. It looks like a delicate Buttercup but it is more lemony yellow than the rich butter yellow of the Buttercup. The petals are thinner and longer and the cup shape is not so pronounced. As the flowers age, they pale to white and they have the ability to close up in cold, darker conditions. The leaves are heart-shaped and occasionally they are slightly variegated.

Apart from producing lots of little seeds per seed head, they also produce tiny tubers in among their roots, which look like miniature potatoes, or the small brown cocoons that one sees if an ant's nest is disturbed. It can therefore spread very quickly. These small root tubers can be collected and roasted and eaten, although you would need a lot to make a snack. All parts of Celandine are said to be edible, but they must be cooked as the fresh material is poisonous.

There are four subspecies of Celandine. Their names have changed over the years but the current scientific name of the species is *Ficaria verna*. The two common and most encountered woodland sub-species are *Ficaria verna Ssp fertilis;* and *Ficaria verna Ssp verna*, the latter of which produces small pale ovoid or elongated tubers in the leaf axils which detach and produce new plants. In the case of *Ssp fertilis* most of the seeds develop fully.

Another minor difference between the two sub-species is that *fertilis* usually has fuller flowers with larger petals and grows throughout Britain, whereas *verna* has narrower petals, which favours woods in eastern Britain and prefers shadier conditions.

Celandine was once believed to be a remedy for haemorrhoids and was thus known as 'pilewort'.

It is also high in vitamin C and was used to prevent scurvy.

GREEN HELLEBORE

Helleborus viridis

Green Hellebore is fairly rare in the wild although many people are familiar with the garden Hellebores, one of which is referred to as Christmas Rose. The garden plants produce flowers of varying colours from yellows through greens, pinks and purples. The wild woodland species has pastel green flowers. It flowers early in the year in February.

When, later in the year, the seeds begin to develop, they are exactly the same shape as the individual seeds that make up the seed heads found on Buttercups, only much larger. The plant is in the same family of *Ranunculaceae*.

This species has been grown in gardens since Medieval times. It was often used as a medicinal herb and can sometimes be found close to the ruins of old houses, monasteries and abbeys. There are some growing near the ruins of Lancaut Church on the banks of the River Wye. It is quite likely that the plants there were planted in the vicinity of the church several hundred years ago. The Green Hellebore is however poisonous and if eaten will cause vomiting. When it was used as a medicinal herb years ago it was used to rid children of worms! It was also rubbed into their hair to rid them of head lice.

Green Hellebore will only grow where the soil is based on lime or is alkaline, so that restricts its range. It is largely found in the south of Britain and there are very few records of sightings in Scotland.

There is some debate about whether *Helleborus viridis* is native or naturalised. There is another plant, *Helleborus occidentalis* which was once regarded as a form of *viridis* but which now stands as a distinct species in its own right. *H. occidentalis* grows more in the north and west than *viridis* and its distribution spreads from Britain across to France, Spain and Germany. *Helleborus occidentalis* is thought to be native and is even more rare than the *Helleborus viridis*.

It can be unclear whether a species is native or just naturalised and I suspect that it really does not matter. They are simply wild flowers and as long as they do not become invasive and out-compete other species, then good luck to them.

Green Hellebore

DOG'S MERCURY

Mercurialis perennis

Dog's Mercury appears early in the year and can be in flower by the end of February. The flowers are not spectacular, but green or yellow, small and formed in loose bunches. There are male and female flowers which are borne on different plants. Apart from seeds, these plants can also reproduce via underground rhizomes. A large patch of Dog's Mercury is likely to be just one individual plant which has spread out by virtue of the rhizomes slowly creeping through the soil. Each patch or plant may be hundreds of years old, as the Dog's Mercury plants often outlive the trees growing above them. The male flowers have tiny little anthers and are easier to spot because they are generally held up above the leaves where presumably the wind can pick up the pollen and distribute it.

The female flowers are more difficult to see as they are tucked down between the leaves and the stem. They are white and feathery and the stigma, which is about all that is visible, is bifid ie. split into two.

Dog's Mercury is a typical woodland plant in that it can tolerate quite a lot of shade but it can also sometimes be found growing in hedgerows, particularly if the hedge is an ancient one and a remnant of former woodland. True woodland species have adapted to the lower light conditions found in the woods in various ways.

Dog's Mercury exhibits two special adaptations particularly well. If light is a limiting factor then it stands to reason that making itself more capable of collecting what little light is available is an advantage. Light collection is carried out by the chlorophyll molecule which is contained in the chloroplasts and Dog's Mercury can increase both the number of chloroplasts per cell and the amount of chlorophyll in each chloroplast. This makes the leaves a darker green. Plants that are growing in the most shady places of a wood will generally be the darkest green.

In a woodland which has been coppiced in the last few years, one will see that Dog's Mercury plants growing right beside the old stump of the coppice will be much darker than plants growing a foot or so out from it, as clearly the closer to the stool (stump), the more shady the conditions. These plants growing closest to the stool will also generally be taller and have bigger leaves. This is because bigger leaves yield better light-gathering potential and a taller plant enables it to out-compete its shorter neighbour.

Dog's Mercury

Many woodland plants show various adaptations to overcome a lack of light, so when light is not a limiting factor, the plant will grow to its average height and have average-sized leaves. As light becomes limited, the plant grows taller and develops bigger leaves but this cannot go on for ever, otherwise just before it got pitch black the plant would have developed into some enormous 'trifid' with leaves like rhubarb.

So there comes a point where, despite having grown taller and increased its leaf size, the plant is receiving only just enough light to just stay alive. This is known as the 'compensation point' and if the light fades below this level, then there is nothing more the plant can do about it and if the conditions endure or get worse, then the plant will die. So any plants growing under a fallen tree, for example, and thus in a shadier place, are considerably larger than those growing in the open.

Dog's Mercury is very tolerant of low light intensities, as is Wood Sorrel.

By the end of May, the seeds will start to develop and be clearly visible.

The name Dog's Mercury is interesting. Mercury is a poison and dogs will often eat a small amount of this plant which will quickly cause them to be sick, enabling them to bring up any fur which may have accumulated in their stomachs as a result of licking themselves.

There are various accounts of dogs eating this plant. I used to have a Springer Spaniel which would sometimes eat some leaves and then a few minutes later be sick. It did not seem to do her any harm, but whether it did any good I do not know.

Possibly another explanation for the name of this woodland plant is that there is another species of Mercury called Annual Mercury which is reputed to be edible, so it could be 'Dog's' because it is *not* edible, in the same way in which Dog Violet does *not* have a sweet perfume.

Dog's Mercury male flowers

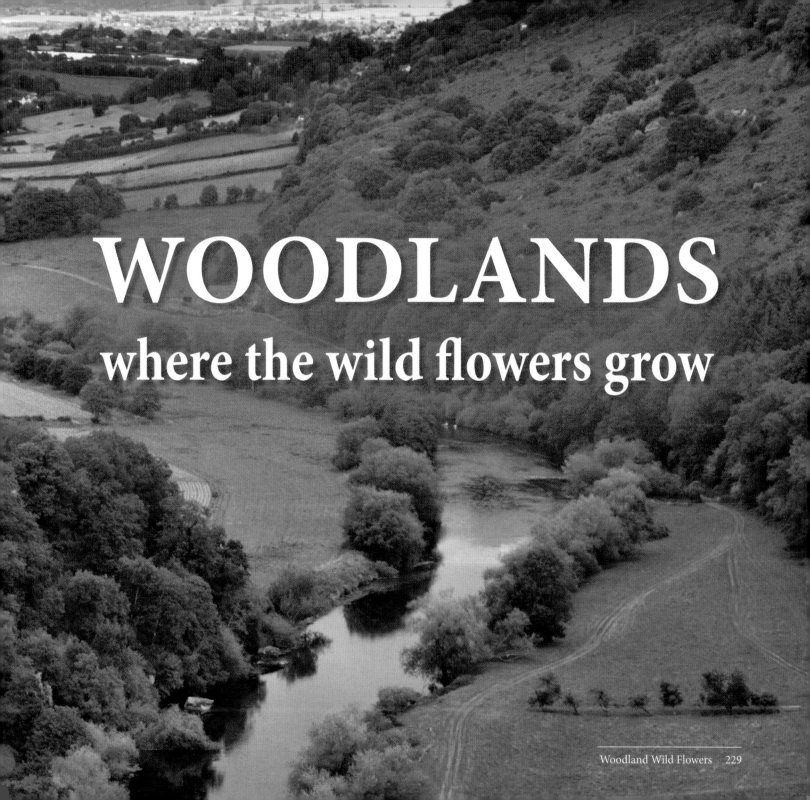

WOODLANDS
where the wild flowers grow

WOODLANDS: WHY THEY LOOK LIKE THEY DO TODAY

We have had several Ice Ages, the last one only about 20,000 years ago. In between each Ice Age, plants and animals recolonised and we have fossils which show that certain trees existed in these inter-glacial periods. Fossilised remains of Silver Fir and Water Chestnut, both of which pre-date the last Ice Age, have been found in Cromer forest beds.

When precisely the last Ice Age came to an end is much debated but the late Professor Oliver Rackham of the historical ecology department, Cambridge University, maintains that *'Woodland history began 12,000 years ago, when the climate became possible for tree growth. Trees and woodland plants returned by wind and bird-borne seed from their southern refugia to form a series of wild-wood plant communities. There followed a long epoch of relative stability, the Atlantic period (6,200–3,800BC) with a climate not very different from that of the mid-twentieth century.'*

Professor Oliver Rackham

It was during this period that modern Britain separated from mainland Europe. There are several items of evidence which give us a fairly good understanding of what happened.

If today one were to travel to northern Siberia or Canada, to the very edge of the ice cap and observe the vegetation, that would almost certainly be what the vegetation looked like in southern England at the end of the last Ice Age. If one were then to walk today in a southerly direction through Canada, one would see the same changes in vegetation as occurred in southern England over a period of several thousand years as the climate gradually warmed up.

One would see first the growth of mosses and lichens mixed with small grasses, heathers, crowberries and maybe a low-growing bush called Creeping Willow: that is to say, a tundra habitat. This habitat does not support trees and the soil is frozen beneath the surface (permafrost). The temperature only exceeds zero degrees centigrade for a few months each year during the summer and even then, below a depth of about 50cm, the soil remains frozen.

Eventually, trees will start to appear as one walks steadily south through Canada, probably Silver Birch, Poplar and Willow. This is the zone (biome) known as *taiga* which extends across the northern hemisphere through Canada, Alaska, Siberia and northern Scandinavia.

Mile by mile as one progresses further south, conifers appear and the forests become more dense. The idea that a closed canopy woodland, like that found in Siberia or Canada, would have developed after the last Ice Age has recently been challenged and possibly a more open patchwork of woodland, scrub and grassland would have arisen. Taiga

Conifer with one- and two-year cones

Beech woodland

is the world's largest land biome, making up 29% of the world's forest cover.

Gradually the prevalence of coniferous trees starts to decline and new deciduous trees such as Oak and Beech make an appearance. One tree that will not be seen much today on the journey south from the Ice Cap will be Elm, because of Dutch Elm disease, but there is evidence that this was one of the early colonisers after the domination of Pines.

Of course, this is only a broad picture and one has to bear in mind that conditions now are not exactly as they were back then. For example one important difference is that the numbers and types of grazing animals present, such as aurochs and tarpana, would have influenced the plant populations.

Further evidence of how woodland developed since the last Ice Age can be found in pollen analysis. Pollen analysis can now be linked with carbon dating to get a better idea of timescale.

Man would have had an increasing effect on woodland even in prehistoric times. In the early years after the end of the last Ice Age, Man was a hunter-gatherer and as such would have had a minimal effect on the woodlands. The human population was tiny and Man was not farming, so there would only have been a small amount of tree felling to provide construction for shelters and for firewood. Man first colonised hilltop sites, because here the trees would have been smaller and more easy to cut down with primitive tools. Furthermore, hilltops offered a more secure position with regard to warding off other tribes and wild animals. Early Man may also have cleared small patches in the woodland to encourage the natural colonisation of plants which provided food such as brambles.

Gradually, around 500 BC, Man became less of a hunter and more of a farmer. This development had a much more dramatic effect on woodlands. Farming hilltops was inefficient because of thin soils and windy, cold conditions so Man shifted his activities down into the valleys. Here he cleared much bigger areas to make little villages and, of course, to create fields to grow crops and in which to keep animals which had been domesticated. The abandoned hilltop sites were still used but largely for sheep grazing, so they developed into moorland, heathland and downs, and did not recover as woodlands.

By the time of the Roman invasion, the English countryside had lost 50 per cent of its woodland and would have looked quite similar to how it looks today in terms of fields, woods and little villages. On the uplands were moors and heaths and

where it was chalky, there was downland. Woodland probably covered only about 10-20% of the land, which is much less than most people would think. It is a common view that there were vast amounts of woodland in the country until quite recently. Legends such as those of Robin Hood have fostered the false notion that swathes of England were made up of deep, dark forests but in fact the proportion of woodland in England 2,000 years ago was about the same as is presently found in France. Most, if not all, of that ancient woodland was either being managed or had been managed at some point, so even then the possibility of 'wild wood' existing is quite remote, 'wild wood' being a woodland that has developed after the last Ice Age, self-perpetuated with natural regeneration and completely unaffected by Man.

During the period of Roman occupation, the population of the country increased, and with it the sophistication of the society. This had significant effects on the amount of woodland remaining. There was charcoal production to provide fuel for local blacksmiths, and large-scale iron production in areas such as the Weald and the Forest of Dean. The Romans were famous for their villas for which bricks were produced along with pottery and tiles, all of which needed kilns which needed charcoal, so by the time the Romans left, the amount of woodland remaining probably below 10%.

The next period through to 1066 was the period of the Anglo Saxons and the Viking invasions. The effect on woodland, as the levels of manufacture prevalent under the Romans decreased, was that the amount of woodland increased – and according to the Domesday Book in the late 11th century, about 15% of the land was wooded.

Over the next 900 years there then followed a steady decline in woodland, as can be seen in this graph.

Woodland as a percentage of land area

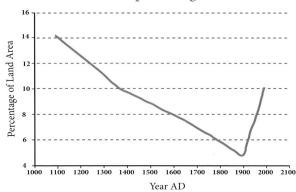

This was caused by a steady population growth and increased demand for farm and grazing land. The later construction of churches, cathedrals and more substantial Tudor houses with big oak beams, along with the development of ships for defence, exploration and trade also used more timber. Eventually the demand for wood started to outstrip the sustainable supply.

SUSTAINABLE WOODLAND: COPPICING

The sustainable method of woodland management, called Coppice-with-Standards, supplied a vast range of materials in an age when, unless wood couldn't do the job, there was only iron, copper and bronze, the production of which was on a relatively small scale. In the coppice system, various species are cut back every few years. They then regenerate and are cut back again and again. This process could go on sustainably for

Ancient coppiced tree ready for the next round of coppicing

Mature Beech

hundreds of years and some species lived far longer under this regime than they would have done if left to grow in a natural way. The regular cutting produces a characteristic stump called a stool, from which the new shoots, known as poles, grow.

I list below a few of the species commonly grown for coppicing and their uses, but most woodland trees and shrubs had some use in the past.

- **Willow** was coppiced on what was perhaps the shortest cycle, of just two or three years. It was used to make woven baskets, fish traps (grigs), beehives (skeps) and fencing material.

- **Hazel** was coppiced on an 8–12-year cycle. The earlier it was cut, the thinner the poles. The majority of it was used to make hurdles, for penning of sheep. Virtually all garments were made from wool or leather so there was a need for lots of sheep. Sheep farming required that sheep be penned together at various times of the year, for lambing and shearing and sometimes for their protection during the winter. Hurdles made strong but temporary enclosures for these activities. The hurdles had a loop at one end and at the other end they were finished off with a pole that stood a few inches higher than the rest of the hurdle. This meant the loop of one could be slotted over the pole of another, and so a long temporary fence could be constructed forming a sort of corral. Hazel was also used for walking sticks.

- **Ash** was coppiced on a long cycle of 15 years or more and had a wide range of uses because it has two good properties: it has a fine grain without too many knots so is easy for a carpenter to work with; and it is flexible, not prone to crack or split. It was therefore used for axes, small farm implements, ploughs and harrows.

In addition, the Coppice-with-Standards woodland provided other essentials for the local community such as firewood, charcoal and food: these woodlands were diverse habitats which supported lots of different edible species such as fungi, fruits and berries, nuts, and herbs for both for medicinal purposes and in cooking. They also encouraged the presence of birds and wild mammals. Acorns were an important source of food for pigs during the winter.

INTER-WAR YEARS

Unfortunately, not all woodland was managed in a sustainable way and the amount of land supporting trees gradually declined, reaching a low point around 1918 at the end of the First World War. Trench warfare had required a lot of wood: planks and posts to maintain the integrity of the trench, duckboards etc. All the wood for the Allies came from Britain and was shipped across to France and Belgium.

FORESTRY COMMISSION

In 1919 the Government set up the Forestry Commission with the brief to purchase land, plant trees and grow them quickly and efficiently in anticipation of a future war, for house building, furniture, pit props and many other uses. At this point the amount of British woodland started to increase and it has steadily risen throughout the last century.

There have been various mishaps along the way. The Forestry Commission has not always been the most popular of bodies, but they *did* meet their brief to produce more timber and to produce it quickly ie. within 40 years. Their solution was Scots Pine, so vast areas of this tree were planted. The nature of Pine plantations is to exclude light so that the trees grow tall and straight: good for telegraph poles and pit props, but it is not the natural way a Scots Pine grows in its native Scotland.

Scots Pines were being planted in regions warmer than Scotland which left the trees vulnerable to a parasitic fungus known commonly as Crown Rot which attacks the topmost shoots and then works its way down, ultimately killing the tree.

As a result, the Forestry Commission switched to planting a similar species, the Corsican Pine, which was also non-native to England, but from a warmer climate. As might be expected, a tree which was not growing in its natural environment was going to be more vulnerable to pests and disease and sure enough another disease came along which attacked the roots and the lower part of the tree. This disease delights in the name Butt Rot. The Forestry Commission managed to control this and continued to plant Corsican Pine but recently another disease called Red Band Needle Blight has appeared. This

Corsican Pines at Ninewells Wood prior to felling

cannot be controlled and is gradually wiping out all Corsican Pines across the country.

As I see it, there is a divide between forestry and woodland management. Forestry involves first and foremost the farming of trees to produce a crop of timber. Over the last generation, the government's directives to the Forestry Commission have changed so that they now have a broader remit which includes conservation, leisure use and education, but timber production is still their primary objective. Woodland management is a far wider concept and takes into account sustainability and biodiversity.

So here we are up to date. Who knows what the state of our woodland will be in 100 or 1,000 years from now? Will we still need wood? Could wood be produced as some sort of tissue culture and not from trees? Will all woodland have to be felled and the land used to produce food?

HOW TO AGE TREES

A woodland walk full of wild flowers could be even further improved, perhaps, by knowing how old those surrounding trees are.

It is possible to tell the age of a tree without cutting it down, but with some tree species it is not possible to determine their age even if they have been cut down. For example, Yew trees can live for thousands of years, but the centre of the trunk starts to break down and the growth rings are no longer discernible.

Some trees can be artificially induced to achieve a great age, for example Ash trees which have been coppiced for many hundreds of years. As the centuries pass, the small branches are cut down to leave a circle of 'units' or stumps known as stools, which moves ever outwards, but the stools were all originally from one tree. You can find five or six coppice stools in a circle, all derived from one 'mother' tree. There is no means of accurately estimating the age but obviously the larger the diameter of the stool, the older it is.

The accurate method of determining the age of a tree is by dendrochronology, that is, counting the rings. The tree does not need to be cut down to do this. A small core can be removed using a special drill, and the rings counted. The diameter of the core taken is only about 3.5mm, and the hole is sealed to stop fungal material getting access. Below is my own collection of tree samples from Ninewells Wood.

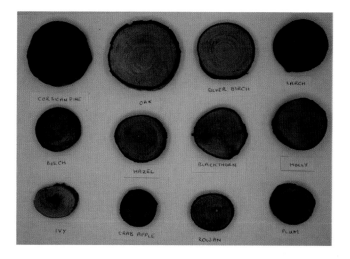

A less accurate method of aging a tree is to measure the girth and the diameter of a tree. The measurement is normally taken at chest height and there are tables available which provide the appropriate factor by which to multiply the diameter in centimetres to get an estimate of the age. The appropriate factor is different for each different species of tree. The factor also varies depending on where the tree is growing because trees growing in the open grow quicker than those growing in dense woodland surrounded by other trees. Poor soil or higher altitude also affect the rate and extent of growth. The Forestry Commission has very detailed and perhaps the most accurate information about tree ageing. A simpler rule of thumb is provided by the National Parks to give at least a reasonable idea of the age.

1. Measure the girth of the tree at shoulder height in centimetres.
2. Divide the girth by the correct number according to the species of tree – *see species in **bold** below.*
3. Round your answer up or down to the nearest whole number. This gives you the approximate age of your tree!

Yew 1.25; Oak 2; Hazel, Elm, Ash, Beech 2.5; Sycamore 2.75; Holly, Pine, Spruce 3.25

Mature Oak perhaps 250 years old.

The list below shows the potential life span in years of some of our most common trees:

Name of tree	Life Span
Alder	120
Ash	200
Beech	350
Birch	100
Cherry	50
Hawthorn	300
Hazel	70
Holly	300
Hornbeam	300
Maple	120
Oak	800
Rowan	120
Scots Pine	500
Willow	400
Yew	3000

POLLEN ANALYSIS

Pollen analysis is a technique which can be used to determine which plants were around thousands of years ago. Pollen has an outer coat (exine) which is incredibly resilient, especially if it is in a constant environment which is either permanently wet or permanently dry.

Different species of plants produce pollen grains with different shapes and different patterns. Some are very distinctive. Pine pollen grains have two little air sacs to help them float on the wind.

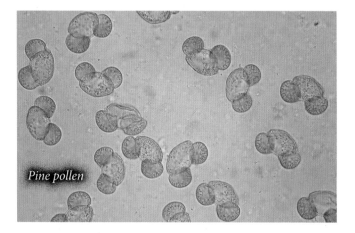

Pine pollen

A good source of pollen grains is to be found in deposits from ancient ponds and lakes. Layers of peat built up from organic matter deposited over thousands of years contain pollen grains released by the plants that were growing at that time. A core sample is taken using a device called a soil auger and the core is then cut into 1cm sections. Each section is older than the one before, as one goes down the core.

The next job, carried out in a laboratory, involves treating each section with hydrofluoric acid which dissolves all the organic material apart from the pollen grains. The excess acid is washed away and what is left are the pollen grains which can be counted and identified under a microscope, revealing which plants or trees were growing at the time the peat was originally formed. There are certain problems. First of all, some species produce more pollen than others. Wind-pollinated species, for

Pollen-rich Hazel catkins

example, produce a great deal of pollen, which can sometimes be seen in Pine woods in spring when a yellow dust coats everything, or in wet woodlands (carr habitats) where ponds develop a yellow scum which is the pollen from Sallow bushes. So a sample which contains 50% Lime pollen and 50% Oak pollen would not indicate that there was a woodland with an equal number of Lime and Oak trees. It would indicate a woodland almost totally dominated by Lime with maybe just one or two Oaks. Lime is partly insect- and partly wind-pollinated, whereas Oak is exclusively wind-pollinated.

Secondly, the pollen in a sample of peat will particularly reflect the species growing closest to the region where the

Pollen grains from different species

peat is forming. Peat is created in a wet area, so the chances of finding pollen from trees such as Alder and Ash which favour damp conditions will be much increased, and the chances of finding Beech or Oak, for example, which favour drier areas, will be much less.

When it comes to smaller woodland plants which may be common in a woodland, such as Bluebells or Ramsons, the amount of pollen produced in comparison to pollen-rich trees such as Silver Birch or Hazel, for example, is minuscule, so finding their pollen grains is more complex, despite them being dominant in the woodland flora. There may well have been lots of grasses growing in historic woodlands, but due to animal grazing, little pollen would have been produced.

Despite these challenges, the overall pollen analysis is a good guide but one which needs careful interpretation. Pollen analysis of ancient woodland provides a sequence of what has occurred, but no dates. Recently carbon dating has been used to work out the ages of each layer in the extracted core with reasonable accuracy so that it is now possible to date the samples.

THE EFFECT OF LIGHT ON WOODLAND

Woodlands create their own special conditions and the plants living there have to adapt to cope with them. Many woodland wild flowers have become so well adapted to this woodland environment that they are rarely found anywhere else. Those plants which are less specialised are more commonly found on the margins of woodland or in open glades and in hedgerows.

By far the most significant environmental factor of a woodland is light.

The light underneath the tree canopy is much less than that outside a woodland. Woodlands vary in density and in the species of trees growing there, and so the range of light energy causes considerable differences. Light is measured in units called lux. Humans can still see easily when there are light levels which are as low as 20 lux, as in the case of a dimly lit room, up to levels of 25,000 lux, which is the case on a bright sunny day. Our eyes are well adapted, so we are not particularly aware of this massive range.

At my Field Study Centre, the students would often carry out investigations into the light levels in different woodlands. Not only is the light in a wood affected by the density and species of trees but in a deciduous woodland it is affected by the seasonal presence or absence of leaves and the number of leaves present.

Light meter

At all times of year, the light inside the woodland is less than the light outside. Even during the winter when there are no leaves on the deciduous trees, there are still twigs and branches which prevent some of the light getting through. As the days get longer and the sun gets higher in the sky in the first three or four months of the year, the leaves start to open. There is still an increase in the amount of light found in the woodland because the daylight hours continue to increase and the strength of the sun continues to strengthen. In early spring the leaves are few, they are small and they have relatively little chlorophyll in them; they have that wonderful light green colour which is not efficient at absorbing light.

As the summer proceeds the leaves get bigger and become a darker green and, more importantly, the trees and bushes grow, with more and more leaves being produced. This increases their light absorption so despite there being more light available, it actually gets darker inside the woods. In the autumn, the leaves fall off the trees and so there is a slight increase in light levels until late autumn and winter.

The woodland plants living underneath the trees - the field layer plants - have to be able to deal with the varying light conditions and there are many strategies which they employ.

It is essential that they make maximum use of the period of the year when most woodland light is available ie. March, April and May. To this end, woodland plants need to get their leaves in position early in the year. It is no good them starting the year as a germinating seedling with two tiny leaves and then steadily growing leaf by leaf because by the time they achieve a reasonable surface area for light absorption, the bright photosynthetic period is over and they will be too late. Woodland plants are therefore mostly perennials which means that they have a large amount of stored-up food in the form of a bulb, corm, tuber, rhizome or swollen root stock. As a result, when the days first start to warm up and the light begins to increase in February then *BANG*, they can convert all that food into leaf; a large amount of fully functional leaf surface which can then make maximum use of the light available in the next three months.

One of the most efficient at doing this is Lords and Ladies (Wild Arum), often

Wild Arum

Wood Anemone leaves going over

the first to push up leaves, even by late January but they are large and easily seen by mid-February. Other plants that are quick out of the blocks are Dog's Mercury and Wood Anemones. The plants with bulbs such as Bluebells and Daffodils are also good exponents of this strategy. Many woodland plants do not bother to retain their leaves after the photosynthetic period is over. One of the first to give up its leaves is the Wood Anemone, which turn yellow and die as early as late May. In a Bluebell wood in July, all that will be seen are lots of white dried up dead leaves lying flat on the ground with the flower stalks still sticking up with ripening seed pods at the top. Some plants such as Dog's Mercury retain their leaves throughout the summer and no doubt they manage to carry out some low level of photosynthesis during this period. The photograph of Wood Anemone leaves was taken in May.

PERENNIAL WOODLAND PLANTS INCREASE THEIR CHANCE OF SURVIVAL

Another reason why most woodland wild flowers are perennials is because an annual plant has to produce sufficient seeds to make sure that at least some seeds will survive and grow the following year, otherwise it would become extinct and it has to do this every year. No second chance. Poppies are annuals and it is estimated that one poppy plant produces up to 60,000 seeds. Foxgloves are biennials and they can produce 7,000 seeds per plant.

7,000 seeds from a single plant

Woodland plants simply do not have enough light energy available in one year to produce this many seeds, so although they do produce them, ideally they do not rely on them. Indeed, many woodland wild flowers only produce seeds every few years, as is the case with many of the orchids. After flowering and producing some seeds, they take a break for a couple of years and build up their food resources, maybe producing another flower a few years later. This may account for the disappearance and then reappearance of some rare woodland species such as the famous Ghost Orchid which has at times been thought to be extinct only to then pop up again.

Becoming perennial is perhaps the most dramatic effect the reduced light has had on woodland wild flowers, but there are other survival devices which many employ. If light is in short supply then making the best use of it is essential, and there are lots of simple things that they can do.

SURVIVAL METHODS FOR WOODLAND PLANTS

• **Large leaves** These are a mixed blessing. They absorb more light, but they lose more water which is why desert plants have reduced leaves or no leaves. However, in a woodland there is usually a lot of water available and it is often more humid and less windy than outside, so transpiration (water loss) is not such a problem.

An efficient leaf arrangement

SOIL IN THE WOODLAND

There are various ways to analyse woodland soil. A soil profile can be obtained by digging down and producing a mini cliff face so that the different zones, known as horizons, can be viewed. Alternatively, a soil auger, like a giant corkscrew,

A soil profile

- **Lots of leaves** The greater the number of leaves, the more a plant can absorb light.
- **Height** The advantage of growing taller is a competitive thing – get above your neighbour.
- **Staggered leaves on the stem** Any time-lapse film of woodland wild flower leaves shows that they are constantly shifting position to get into brighter places where they are not shaded by leaves above them. They also adjust the angle: a vertical one is most beneficial when the sun is lower in the sky; a more horizontal angle is best when the sun is high in the sky. To aid this, the leaves are generally arranged in a spiral pattern up the stem.
- **Maximised leaf design** to make it more efficient at capturing the limited amount of light.
- **Variable amounts and types of pigment** The chlorophyll is the green substance which absorbs the light. Although chlorophyll absorbs light, it is also sensitive to it and if there is too much light it can be destroyed. In shady woodland, some plants' leaves become darker green which enables it to absorb more light.

These different strategies are employed, sometimes in combination, by various woodland wild flowers. There are many other environmental factors affecting woodland plants such as the quality of the soil, the humidity and the wind, but the single factor which has the most effect is light which is why I have dealt with it in some detail.

can be screwed into the ground to a depth of about 10-15cm. The core of soil is retained on a tray. The soil auger is then placed back into the hole and screwed in to a further depth of 10-15cm and the next layer of soil is detached and retained. This process is repeated several times so that a core of soil is removed and reconstructed on the tray, enabling its structure to be seen.

The pH can be tested, and there are various kits which record nitrate and phosphate levels. These are the most important

A soil auger

Beech in the Forest of Dean

nutrients in the soil but it is also possible to test for other minerals such as potassium or iron. Water levels can also be ascertained and to do this, a sample large enough to fill a petri dish is needed. It is then a matter of weighing it fresh, drying it out and reweighing it. The decrease in weight represents the amount of water present which can then be converted into a percentage of the whole.

Usually a woodland soil profile shows a narrow layer at the top consisting of leaf litter, followed by a thin layer of organic debris in which remnants of leaves and twigs can still be made out. This merges into a dark, rich layer where organic matter and soil blend. Below this we often find a build-up of rocky particles and stones before getting down to the bedrock.

What this all means for woodland plants is that the surface is rich and well supplied with nutrients, so surface rooting is a good idea. Tree roots penetrate deeper to gain stability but most woodland plants restrict their root mass to a layer which is no more than 50cm deep.

The pH of the soil is also important, and it is usual to test soil samples from different depths of maybe 5, 20, 35 and 50cm. The pH level affects the type of trees which will grow in a given area. Oaks grow on soil with a lower pH whereas Beech prefers where it is higher.

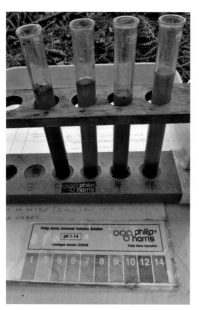

Some woodland wild flowers such as the calcifuges, will only grow where the pH is below seven, ie. acidic. I like to think of calcifuges as plants seeking refuge from calcium! Examples of these are Heather and Bilberry. Others favour an alkaline pH (chalky) and these are called calcicoles. Examples of these include a number of the orchids.

In woodland soils, the constant input of dead leaves every autumn creates a layer of leaf litter which gradually decomposes, producing leaf mould, an organic-rich layer. Beneficial though this is, it is acidic, as leaves contain chemicals such as tannins which are mild acids. As a result, anywhere where a woodland has been in existence for more than a few years will have a soil pH lower than the surrounding areas on which there is no woodland. It could lower the pH by one or two on the scale. And conifers tend to make the pH lower than deciduous trees do.

The next most important quality of the soil is the water content, which varies depending on whether the soil is clay or a more open soil (loam). If the soil is wet, trees such as Alder and Ash will be favoured. Drier soils tend to favour Silver Birch. The layer of leaf litter is beneficial in maintaining a good water level. The leaf litter holds water but has air spaces, so it is damp but not waterlogged.

Woodland soils will tend to be rich in nutrients, especially nitrates and phosphates, because of the breakdown of the leaf litter by small invertebrates, fungi and micro-organisms.

Finally, woodland soils tend to be slightly warmer than other soils and again this is a product of the leaf litter and humus when decomposition produces heat. In addition, warmth enters the soil via air spaces and this layer will have lots of air spaces in the leaf litter.

AIR TEMPERATURE AND WIND IN WOODLANDS

All that remains are the effects of air. Woodland air temperature is more steady than the temperature outside a woodland. In the winter it is warmer in a wood and in the summer it is cooler. This favours both plants and animals. The air is also always more damp in a wood than outside it, partly as a result of evaporation from the moist leaf litter layer and partly as a result of transpiration from the leaves. Wind speed is lower in a wood than outside, because the leaves and branches slow the air flow.

TYPES OF WOODLAND

Spinney, copse, grove, wood and forest are all names that one associates with places containing trees and many might think that the terms simply refer to relative sizes, a forest being larger than a wood and so on. A spinney is often described as a small copse, although I tend to think of a spinney as being an area planted or used by gamekeepers to attract pheasants. I also think of a grove as consisting of a long narrow band of trees.

Various types of woodland

Forest was a term originally introduced to England by the Normans and it denoted a large area which would include wooded regions, open fields and parkland which provided suitable habitats for deer and other game. It was quite possible therefore to be in a forest and not be surrounded by trees. The origin of the word dates back to Emperor Charlemagne who used the latin '*forestis silva*' for his hunting grounds.

When William the Conqueror formally established his first 'forests' in Britain, originally there were about 25 of them, eventually growing to number about 80. The New Forest was one of the first.

Many of these forests included land which was not wooded, such as the Forest of Bowland today, but gradually the name came to mean a wooded area and eventually the word was used entirely in that context, as it was with the formation of the Forestry Commission in 1919.

ANCIENT WOODLAND

Other terms one regularly comes across in woodland literature are **Original Woodland, Wild Wood** and **Ancient Woodland**. Original and Wild Wood are the same thing. Both terms refer to woodland which developed after the last Ice Age and which has been in existence ever since. The essential characteristic is that the wood should have remained throughout that time unaffected by Man, so there is to have been no felling, no planting of selected trees and no coppicing. There is no original woodland left in Britain, and probably none left in western Europe. The Białowieża Forest in Poland and areas across Russia and Canada probably qualify but one can never know for sure what has happened in the past.

Ancient Woodland is defined as woodland which has been in existence since 1600 AD in England and Wales and since 1750 AD in Scotland. The thinking is that if it was there in 1600 then it had probably been there for a longer time prior to that date so it was likely that a woodland had existed on that site ever since the last Ice Age or it may have been cleared at some stage in pre-history but then naturally regenerated and been in existence ever since. This does not mean that Man will not have had some influence on its history. Many woods were managed in the past as Coppice-with-Standards.

The Forestry Commission has introduced some subdivisions to the definition of ancient Woodland.

Ancient Semi-Natural Woods (ASNW) are those which have native species but may have been managed and thus modified by Man over many years.

Plantations on Ancient Woodland Sites (PAWS) are Ancient Woodland sites which have been cleared at some stage and then planted with non-native species, often just one species such as Corsican Pine. The portion of Ninewells Wood which we purchased in 2015 was a PAWS site.

Recovering Ancient Woodland Site (RAWS) is what our own woodland has become, because we felled all the Corsican Pines and have replaced them with native species, all carried out under supervision from the Forestry Commission authorities. In our case this has been achieved in three ways. A lot of Silver Birch has grown up naturally, along with a few other species such as Rowan and Holly. In addition, I planted hundreds of acorns, most of which provided nourishment for local wildlife, but a percentage did survive and grow. I also grew various native species of tree at home, protected in little pots until they were a couple of years old and then planted them out, protected at this stage with plastic sleeves. The trees which I cultivated were Oak, Beech and Hazel.

All woodland varies according to the type of soil, whether it is acidic or alkaline, light or heavy, how wet it is and the depth of soil. The local temperature and humidity will also have an effect. Ancient Woodlands also vary depending on proximity to the coast and whether it is in the south, west, north or east of Britain. All these factors conspire to produce different mixes of tree and shrub species, which have been classified into a complex system. Those who visit a woodland or own a woodland might like to consider what type of woodland it is. There are officially 19 different categories of woodland, and six other related habitats.

HEDGES

In a book about woodland wild flowers it is appropriate to say a little about hedgerows. After all a hedgerow is really a very long and very narrow woodland, more so if it also contains a few trees. Its lack of width means that more light will be available to the wild flowers growing beneath it but in some situations the available light can be quite similar to that in certain regions of woodland. For example the north side of a tall hedge which is aligned east to west can compare to a boundary bank on the south side of a woodland.

The woodland wild flowers I have included in this book are not just true 100% woodland species but also most of the shade-tolerant species which can be found growing in fairly open woodlands, and therefore hedgerows too.

The original hedge was often formed during the Bronze Age, when woodland clearance took place and a narrow strip of the original woodland was left between one cleared area and another. These hedges, having formed part of a woodland, would naturally contain its wild flowers. Gradually the hedgerows have been infiltrated by what are now considered to be typical hedgerow species such as Cow Parsley, Hogweed and Campion.

There are some hedges in Norfolk just north of Swaffham which contain the woodland wild flower Dog's Mercury and Bluebells, so these hedges are probably examples of remnant woodland hedges.

But most hedgerows today are not the remnants of Ancient Woodland. There are two ways in which modern hedgerows can be formed. One is by the planting of a row of trees and bushes. The preferred species in these cases were often those with thorns and prickles as they rendered the hedge more impenetrable. Species such as Hawthorn and Blackthorn were often 'layed' although no doubt a landowner would sometimes just uproot shrubs and tree seedlings from the neighbourhood and plant these in a row, thereby achieving an instant hedge.

The other way a modern hedge can be created is by the erection of a fence, be it of posts and wire or wood. Over a period of time, birds sit on the fence and their droppings may well contain viable seeds contained in what the bird has been eating, such as Blackberry seeds, Sloe stones, Rose hip seed or Hawthorn seeds. These seeds then germinate directly under or next to the fence, grow up and produce a hedge, with the old fence located in the centre. Over time the old fence rots, so that a hundred years later there will be a hedge and no sign of the original fence.

One can tell how old a hedge is by counting the number of woody species growing in it. The more there are, the older it

is. The thinking behind this is that if a hedge is planted using just one species, Hawthorn for example, then over time the original individuals will die and something else will grow in its place. This is most likely to be another Hawthorn but it could possibly be a different species, and gradually over the centuries the hedge originally made up of a single species will become more and more diverse.

This general theory has been refined and there are now various formulae which can be used to estimate the age of a hedge, by using old records and maps where a hedge can be fairly accurately pinpointed by the date of the map, and then counting the species that are present in it today. The simple formula is to **count the number of woody species in a 30 yard section; each different species adds another 100 years to the age**. However, caution needs to be exercised in reaching conclusions.

Wood Anemone, a strong Ancient Woodland Indicator

ANCIENT WOODLAND INDICATOR SPECIES

Certain woodland wild flowers, including grasses, sedges and rushes, are known as indicator species. What this means is that if a woodland has several such species growing in it, then it is likely to be ancient. Ancient Woodland is defined as woodland which has been in existence since 1600 AD in England and Wales and since 1750 AD in Scotland. The more indicator species which the woodland contains, the more likely it is to be ancient.

The basis on which a plant gets onto the list largely involves the analysis of plants growing in historically recorded Ancient Woodland sites. Some woodland plants are incredibly slow to spread and cannot rapidly colonise a woodland, so if they are present then it is likely that the woodland is extremely old.

The speed with which species colonise is often governed by the way their seeds are dispersed. Many of the Ancient Woodland indicator species (AWIs) rely on ants to pick up the seeds and move them to a new location. Common Cow-wheat, Wood Anemone, Sweet Violet and Goldilocks Buttercup all use this method. Of these species, some have even developed seeds which look like ant eggs, others have an additional part to the seed called an *elaiosome* which is food for the ant and some produce a smell that attracts them. Clever as all this is, it does mean that the distribution is limited to the distance an ant is able to travel, which is why newly planted woods are unlikely to be colonised by the plants that use this technique. This reliance on ants to effect distribution is known as *myrmechory*. In earlier times when woodlands were more continuous, there was not a problem with this means of distribution but today, with most woodlands being small, isolated blocks split up from one another by roads, railways and buildings, the ants are just not able to bridge the gaps.

Overleaf is my suggested list of Ancient Woodland species. It is based on several other lists by various authorities and my own observations. I have not included any grasses, sedges or rushes as I have not included these groups in this book on woodland wild flowers. I have also omitted mosses and ferns for the same reason. The one exception to this is the grass Wood Mellick, *Mellica uniflora* as this grass is more or less universally regarded as a very strong indicator of ancient woodlands.

Ancient woodland indicator plants

Woodruff *Gallium odoratum*
Wood Anemone *Anemone nemorosa*
Common Cow-wheat *Melampyrum pratense*
Moschatel *Adoxa moschatellina*
Wood Spurge *Euphorbia amygdaloides*
Herb Paris *Paris quadrifolia*
Bird's Nest Orchid *Neottia nidus-arvis*
Climbing Corydalis *Ceratocapnos claviculata*
Wood Sorrel *Oxalis acetosella*
Wood Speedwell *Veronica montana*
Ramsons *Allium ursinum*
Lily of the Valley *Convallaria majalis*
Yellow Archangel *Galeobdolon luteum*
Early Purple Orchid *Orchis mascula*
Pignut *Conopodium majus*
Toothwort *Lathraea squamaria*
Nettle-leaved Bellflower *Campanula trachelium*
Broad-leaved Helleborine *Epipactis helleborine*
Bitter Vetchling *Lathyrus linifolius*
Yellow Pimpernel *Lysimachia nemorum*
Butterfly Orchid *Platanthera chlorantha*
Wood Dog Violet *Viola reichenbachiana*
Violet Helleborine *Epipactis purpurata*
Water Avens *Geum rivale*
Green Hellebore *Helleborus viridis*
Tutsan *Hypericum androsaemum*
Sanicle *Sanicula europaea*
Wood Vetch *Vicia sylvatica*
Columbine *Aquilegia vulgaris*
Figwort *Scrophularia nodosa*
Goldilocks *Ranunculus auricomus*
Meadow Saffron *Colchicum autumnale*
Monkshood *Aconitum napellus*
Solomon's Seal *Polygonatum multiflorum*
Three-nerved Sandwort *Mochringia trinerva*
Wood Forget-me-not *Myostis sylvatica*
Wild Daffodil *Narcissus pseudonarcissus*

Bluebells and Primroses are sometimes quoted as indicator species along with Dog's Mercury but these all seem to regenerate quite easily.

In any particular wood, only a limited number of the above species could possibly exist, because some species are restricted to alkaline soils and others only live on acidic soils. Furthermore some species are only found in the south, as a northern woodland might be too cold to support them.

HUNTING FOR WOODLAND WILD FLOWERS

When deciding to write this book about our woodlands and their wild flowers, I initially identified about 150 wild flowers that I wanted to include. I would need the photographs of these plants and then I would write about them. I already had many photographs of wild flowers taken over the years, but there were others which I had to search out. It took about two years to find and photograph the majority of plants included in this book and I was eventually left with about thirty species still to locate.

There are four lines of attack which I employ when trying to find a plant.

- The first is to use the resources offered by the Botanical Society of Britain and Ireland (BSBI). On their website one can type in the name of a particular plant and then zoom in on their map and see where the plants may be found in any given ten kilometre square or hectad. These are subdivided into tetrads which are two kilometres square. However, even two kilometres is quite a large area if one is looking for a plant that is only 10cm tall.
- The second step is to refer to local books which give plant locations. Even if they are well out of date, they do still help.
- Thirdly there are the Naturalist Trusts which have records of what has been seen, and these records are up to date. However they do tend to reflect the location of their members as much as the distribution of the plants.
- Another useful resource is the internet and particularly a

Quite old but still useful

Facebook group called Wild Flowers of Britain and Ireland which has over 20,000 members. By keeping an eye on this, one can be alerted to a particular plant that one is looking for. However that can then result in a long journey.

THE ORIGIN OF PLANTS' NAMES

Wild flowers have two names: a common name and a scientific name. They may, and often do, have a number of common names but they only have one scientific name and this name will be the same the world over.

The system of using scientific names, known as the binomial system, was introduced by Linnaeus otherwise known as Carl von Linné, in 1765. Each species, whether plant or animal, was given two scientific names. Its first name denotes its genus and the second its species. The first name always starts with a capital letter and the second always with a lower-case letter so, for example, we have *Ranunculus repens*. Here the name denotes that it is a type of Buttercup *Ranunculus* and that the specific species is the Creeping Buttercup.

There are often several species in each genus so there is also *Ranunculus acris*, *Ranunculus bulbosus* and so on. In fact there are hundreds of species in this genus and they are found all over the world.

The advantage of this system is that a botanist in any part of the world will use the same scientific name for each species so if one referred to *Ranunculus repens* when talking to a Chinese botanist, he or she would know what was being referred to, as would an Albanian or an Icelander.

Scientific names have advantages but they lack the romanticism of the common names. Many of these were invented by some of the great botanists of the past, including William Turner between 1538 and 1548, and Henry Lyte in his *Nieue Herball* or *Historia of Plants* 1578.

There were reasons for the common 'folk' names of, for example, Milkmaids, Cuckooflower or Lady's Smock, some quite surprising. There is fascination in the uses to which the plant has been put in the past, in whether its population is increasing or decreasing and then there is one's own personal encounters with a plant, all of which add up to make a plant more interesting.

Quite a few common names, such as Bluebell or Buttercup, have an obvious origin because they describe the flower. Others describe a plant's habitat as in the case of the Wallflower or Field Clover. Then there are names which relate to the shape of a plant's leaves as in Pennywort or Ragwort. As many people know, the name Dandelion is a reference to the leaves, which are jagged and shaped like a

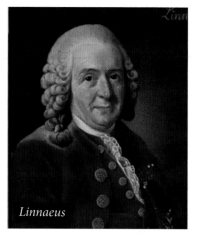

Linnaeus

Meadowsweet

lion's teeth, hence in French *Dent de Lion*. This is one of the many plant names that result from the Norman conquest, but it was the Anglo Saxons living in Britain after 1066 who corrupted the French name into Dandelion. I wonder what it was originally called by the Anglo Saxons? Another name for it was 'Devil's Milkpail'. There is another French name for this plant, *Pissenlit*, because it is reputed to cause bedwetting in children if eaten.

Other common names relate to either culinary or medicinal use of wild flowers and these include names like Nipplewort, so named for its perceived benefit for lactating mothers.

Many plant names end with 'wort' which derives from the Anglo Saxon 'wyrt' which means 'root'.

Asphodel has a Greek origin and became corrupted to Affodel and thence to Daffodil.

There are some names which are more complicated than they first appear. For example Meadowsweet sounds fairly obviously a reference to a sweet smelling flower which grows in meadows but this is not the case. It gets its name because it was added to Mead to sweeten the flavour, thus it was Meadsweet. In German it is known as Madesuss and it was formerly known as meadowyrt from *medu*, mead; and *wyrt*, plant or root.

To sum up, an interest in woodland wild flowers is an absorbing hobby which can lead from simple identification to travelling to find elusive ones, to photography, to historic research, to etymology and onwards, and it can last an absorbing lifetime.

GLOSSARY

Acidic – a pH lower than seven

Alkaline – a pH greater than seven

Annual – plant with a one-year life cycle

Anther – the male organ containing pollen, part of a stamen

Axil – junction between the leaf and the stalk

Biennial – plant with a two-year life cycle

Biotype – a group of organisms within a species sharing the same genetic make-up

Bract – leaf-like appendage often just below a flower head

BSBI – Botanical Society of Britain and Ireland

Bulbil – small bulb-like organ sometimes produced in the axil instead of a flower

Calcicole – plant which grows in alkaline areas

Calcifuge – plant growing in acidic areas

Calyx – ring of sepals

Capitulum – a flower head where the individual flowers are tightly packed together with no visible individual stalks

Capsule – a dry fruit made of several segments, as in Poppy

Carpel – female organ of flowering plants comprising stigma, style and ovary

Carr – waterlogged wooded terrain

Calcareous/calciferous – containing calcium carbonate. Chalky soil, or limestone areas

Chlorophyll – green plant pigment used for photosynthesis

Chloroplast – disc-shaped cell organelle containing chlorophyll

Cladode – a green leaf-like shoot, as in Butcher's Broom

Cleistogamous – mechanism for self-pollination where the flower does not open e.g. some violets

Creeping Buttercup

Compositae – large family of flowers with daisy-like structures

Coniferous – trees producing seeds in cones

Coppice – woodland management technique whereby trees and bushes are cut back regularly to produce new growth

Coppice-with-Standards – woodland habitat with a mixture of coppiced and fully grown mature trees (standards)

Corm – swollen stem base for food storage/overwintering

Corolla – whorl of petals forming a tube e.g. as in Daffodil

Cowl – upper hood-like petal e.g. Monkshood

Crenellated – leaf margin with rounded indentations

Cultivar – a variety artificially produced by cultivation

Cuticle – surface layer of leaf

Deciduous – plants which lose their leaves in the autumn

Dioecious – species with male and female flowers on different plants e.g. Campion

Dothistroma – disease affecting pines also known as red band needle blight

Elaiosome – fleshy structures attached to seeds of some plant species to attract ants

Epidermis – outer layer of cells on leaves stems and roots

Filament – stalk of an anther

Florets – a small flower which is part of a compound head

Gall – a swelling on leaves or flowers caused by insects which live inside it

Gametes – haploid sex cells e.g. anthrazoids, oospheres, pollen and ovules

Hectad – a unit of 10km x 10km square.

Honeyguide – markings on the petals to direct pollinating insects to the nectar

Humus – decomposing organic matter in the soil

Hybrid – a species originating by the fertilisation of one species by another

Internodal – the region between nodes (joints) on plant stems

Lanceolate – a leaf shape resembling a lance

Lobed leaf – a deeply toothed leaf not subdivided into individual leaflets

Lux – unit of measurement of light

Myrmecochory – seed dispersal carried out by ants

Nectary – part of flower producing nectar

Node – stem joint where leaves are attached

Nutlet – a small nut, as on the surface of a Strawberry

Ovary – part of the flower containing the ovules

Palmately lobed – leaf shape resembling a hand with fingers

Parasite – organism relying entirely on another organism for its sustenance

PAWS – ancient woodland sites where the semi-natural woodland has been replaced with a plantation

Perennial – plant living for many years, surviving each winter by storing food in corms, bulbs or tubers

Petiole – leaf stalk which attaches the leaf to the stem

pH – a measure of acidity/alkalinity

Pheromone – chemical released by an animal for detection by another of the same species

Phyllotaxis – movement of leaves e.g. to seek better light conditions

Pole – a narrow trunk produced by coppicing

Pollinia – modified detachable anther found in orchids

Propagation – producing new offspring

RAWS – forestry term for Recovering Ancient Woodland site

Rhizome – modified stem which grows through or just above the soil used for propagation and/or overwintering

Rostellum – part of an orchid flower to which pollinia are attached

Saprophyte – plant deriving nutrition from dead remains e.g. some fungi

Sepals – leaf-like appendages often used to protect the flower whilst in bud

Spadix – the upright core in Arum lilies producing a smell to attract pollinating insects

Spathe – hood surrounding spadix found in Arum lily

Spur – tube-like extension containing nectar at the base of some flowers

Stamen – male reproductive organ in flower comprising anther and filament

Standard – fully-grown mature tree, used to provide large timber

Stellate – star-like

Stigma/stigmatic surface – the part of a carpel on which pollen is deposited

Stomata – pore on the underside of a leaf

Stolon – stem modified to aid asexual reproduction, as in strawberries

Stool – the base of a coppiced tree or bush

Style – the stalk coming from the carpel at the end of which the stigma is located

Tendril – a twisted filament rising from a leaf or stem used for climbing

Tepal – a flower part which combines the sepal and the petal, as in the Anemone

Tetrad – an area 2 km x 2 km square.

Transpiration – the evaporation of water from a leaf

Trifoliate – leaf subdivided into three leaflets e.g. Clover

Tuber – a stem modified for storing food and thus overwintering e.g. potato

Umbel – compound flower head producing a platform of flowers closely arranged together

Umbellifer – a plant in the carrot family producing umbels

Whorl – a group of leaves or petals all arising from the same point, as in Bedstraws

Wild Strawberry

INDEX OF COMMON NAMES

Yellow Pimpernel

INDEX OF SCIENTIFIC NAMES

Also published by Merlin Unwin Books

Wild Flowers of Britain: month by month Margaret Erskine Wilson

My Wood Stephen Dalton

Wildlife of the Pennine Hills Doug Kennedy

A Kaleidoscope of Butterflies Jonathan Bradley

Hedgerow Medicine Julie Bruton Seal & Matthew Seal

The Forest of Bowland Helen Shaw

...and many more. Full details of all our countryside books on:

www.merlinunwin.co.uk